THE HOUSE THAT JESUS BUILT

THE EMERGING REVIVAL, REFORMATION, AND RESTORATION

KEN MULLIS

The House that Jesus Built

Copyright © 2019 by Ken Mullis
All rights reserved.

Published in Houston, Texas by Battle Ground Creative
First Edition

Softcover: 978-1-947554-95-5
RELIGION / Christian Life / Spiritual Growth

Battle Ground Creative is a publishing company with an ephasis on helping first-time authors find their voice. Named after an obscure city in Washington State, we currently operate offices in Houston, Texas and Philadelphia, Pennsylvania. For a complete title list and bulk order information, please visit www.battlegroundcreative.com.

Unless otherwise noted, scripture quotations are taken from The New King James Version®. Copyright © 1982 by Thomas Nelson. Used by Permission. All rights reserved.

Scripture quotations marked "NIV" are taken from THE HOLY BIBLE, NEW INTERNATIONAL VERSION®, NIV®. Copyright 1973, 1978, 1984, 2011 by Biblica, Inc.® Used by permission. All rights reserved worldwide.

Edited by: Jared Stump
Cover design: Tessa Mullis
Cover artwork: Travis Binish
Interior design and typeset: Katherine Lloyd
Printed in the United States of America

DEDICATION

I dedicate this book first and foremost to my faithful heavenly Father who I love, a Father who would not let me go. To the Son of God as well, who demonstrated the love of our Father in and through the work of the cross that He endured; the Son who gave us the first glimpse of our Father's heart. Also, to the Holy Spirit, who relentlessly pointed me to Jesus when I have wanted to look away, whose magnificent works are beyond our imagination. Yes, the Spirit of God who is near the brokenhearted and downtrodden. To God be the glory, forever and ever.

I also dedicate this book to the brokenhearted, the poor, the sick, the downtrodden, and the weak, particularly those who don't have any fight left in them. The losers, the misfits, the confused, the imprisoned ones, the disenfranchised, and those who are poor in spirit. The abused, hurt, bruised, traumatized, and crushed. The sinner, the forgotten, the overlooked, the shunned, the ostracized, and the judged. To the conflicted, afflicted, addicted, and convicted. To those with thorns, and those who simply know they need grace or they won't make it. To those who don't wear their successes, position, authority, or their hardships like a badge of honor or a rite of passage. To those who are desperately looking for a Savior, for they will surely find Him, because those are the ones He came for. To the remnant, the tender of heart, the meek and the peacemakers. To whosoever will hear what the Spirit is saying. This is your book. This is your moment. I bring good news.

Next, I want to honor my family. First, my wife, Christy, who has exercised great patience and faith in being my wife and the mother of our children. She one who I share my contemplations with. To my children as well for all they have had to endure—more than anyone will ever know to this point—for me to follow after God and for this book to become a reality. They have watched me fall and they have watched me rise again. Some, more than once.

I am a thankful man. Only God could make that so. Thank you to everyone who believes in me, and especially for believing in God in me.

CONTENTS

Introduction 1
It's Birthing Time 5
Revival is Born 8
Birthing These Things of the Spirit 12
There are Two Houses in our Garden 15
Revival and the Restoration of All Things 19
An Enemy of Revival 25
Revival, Reformation, Restoration, and the Elijah Commission 28
The Circumcision 33
   A Word to My Prophets 39
   A Warning to False Prophets 40
A Scriptural and Prophetic Description of Revival and Reformation . . . 41
The Present Reformation, Concerning the Church 46
The Present Reformation, Concerning Apostles 49
   A Word to My Apostles 56
   The Apostle 59
Why Was Jesus Sent? 62
What is a Cornerstone? 65
   A Vision and Word Concerning the Cornerstone 67
The Army of the Lord 70
There is Only One Body 74
The Most Precious Gift Ever Given 77
We Must Be in Love 79
The Intellect 82

A Key to Hearing God's Voice 83
The Enemy of Reformation 86
The Enemy of Our Souls 88
    Ode of the Enemy 88
Personal Accounts 90
Prophetic Words of Revival, Reformation, and Restoration 95
    The Passing of Billy Graham — February 2018 95
    Revival with No Ebb — March 4, 2018 98
    The Generation of Restoration — January 30, 2015 100
    Keys, Open Doors, Prison Breaks, Recompense, Reformation,
    and Restoration — February 23, 2018 101
    A Word to All who are Called by My Name —
    March 11, 2018 104
Keys to Revival 106
Mary and Martha 107
He Loves You Above Your Abilities 110
    Growing Up in Christ 111
Mothers and Fathers 114
Do Not Seek the Honor that Comes from Men 118
Submission to Authority 122
Do Not Be Swayed by the Crowd 124
The Process 126
The Purpose in the Pain 128
God Sees Your Tears 132
    Enduring Whispers in the Night 133
Going Lower Still 135
I Know What It's Like 136
    It Was On the Road to Jericho 138

Being Content 141
Rest Reveals Our Faith 144
The Illegitimate and Unlikely 145
A Failed Test to Remember 147
A Shocking and Pleasant Surprise 149
Cheer Others On 152
The Confrontational Christ 154
The Heart of Jesus 159
Don't Shoot the Architects 161
A Word to Artists 163
    The Artisan 166
A Word to My Chosen Ones and Their Scoffers 168
The Secret Place 170
A Profound Mystery 173
    He IS 175
Conclusion 177
Special Thanks 181
About the Author 183

INTRODUCTION

I am excited about this book. Not so much because I wrote it, but because of the events that took place over a lifetime to harvest the content.

It was a Wednesday, in the spring of 1997, when I had an extraordinary encounter with the Lord. We were struggling to make ends meet, and I was lying across my bed, praying, when I heard the words, *Sell all you have and follow Me.*

I jumped up and went to my wife, Christy, to tell her what I thought I just heard. In typical Christy fashion, she said, "Let's do it!" In typical Ken fashion, I said, "Well, now, let's be sure!"

Later that day, a good friend named Fred McKinnon gave me a call. Fred was the worship leader at Christian Renewal Church on Georgia's St. Simons Island. He told me they were hosting a night of worship that Friday night and he wanted us to attend.

Friday afternoon, Christy and I were on our way down to the island. At one point, I told her, "You know, if I knew God was really saying to sell what I have and follow Him, I would do it. But I'm concerned because my parents and your grandmother are getting older and I want them to get to spend time with their grandchildren. Nevertheless, if that is what we are to do, I will go."

That night, at Fred's church, we had a wonderful time in worship. A couple of hours had passed, and I felt it was winding down when Fred said, "I still think God wants to do something else before we go."

About that time, a lady in the back of the room stood up and prophetically said, "So, you really want to sell all you have and follow me?

Well, I've heard your 'yes,' and I am going to sanctify your 'yes,' but you are going to have to let the dead bury the dead!"

Uh-oh, that was us! Then, another lady, one of the singers (who I later found out was the pastor's wife) walked up to me and said, "God's promises are yes and amen concerning you!"

As you can imagine, the tears began to fall. I was awestruck at how quickly God had confirmed His word.

The next day, I was watching T.D. Jakes on television, and he began preaching about David being anointed by Samuel to be king. While he was preaching this message, I began to feel as though oil was being poured over my head. Wave after wave came over me, and I was doubled over with deep heaves and groans pouring out of me. This went on and on. Even into the night, I would double over. I felt like I was getting a heavenly download too big to comprehend, and I was. I felt like I was being purged and filled at the same time. The next day was Sunday, and I was still experiencing the episodes over and over into the night.

Monday morning came, and I had to go to work at 6:00 am with the sheriff's office, where I was a sergeant with the patrol division. I decided to stop by and eat breakfast at my mom and dad's house on the way to work. As I was telling them what had happened to me, I began speaking prophetically. I saw stadiums filled with folks crying out to God. There was a tremendous power on the spoken word, and many of the people in the crowd could not stand under the weight of it. God was touching the masses in a way I had never seen before. I believed what was happening to me was going to happen on a massive scale; I was tangibly experiencing what those in the stadiums were going to experience. I prophesied these things for about forty-five minutes as my mother's tears bore witness to what was coming out of my mouth.

After this, I received a call that I was needed at the office. As I was getting in my car, I heard, *Prepare the way of the Lord! Prepare the way of the Lord! Prepare the way of the Lord!* It was not an audible voice, but loud in my heart. I could not process what I was receiving because it was too

INTRODUCTION

much for my simple mind. This is why I am grateful that God does not just speak to our minds, but to our hearts.

This event lasted well through Tuesday before it slowly began to wane. I knew I had encountered a supernatural God. I had received an impartation and a taste of things to come. This experience was truly more than I could comprehend or articulate. In fact, much of what I believe was imparted to me from this experience seemed to be locked up on the inside of me for many years. This experience would become the catalytic force and shift that would send my family and I on a journey of some extreme life experiences and discovery. What was imparted through this experience has been a developing picture over the last two decades.

Fast forward twenty-one years. On February 14, 2018, a prophet by the name of Jeff Jansen came to minister at the Ramp Church. During the service he turned toward me, looked me in the eye, and made a motion as though he were sticking a key in my belly and turning it. This was followed later that night by a prophetic word of a promised future from the Lord. In fact, Jeff Jansen and Karen Wheaton Towe both prophesied over us. Our spirits were deeply stirred.

That night after church while sitting around our dinner table, I was reminding Christy and one of my sons, Josiah, of the events that had taken place in the spring of 1997. Christy had lived those events with me, but Josiah had not yet been born when this happened; he was hearing the details for the first time. We had been invited to hear Jeff Jansen speak again the next morning as he ministered at The Ramp School of Ministry.

When Jeff Jansen came out on the platform the next morning, he began by giving an account from when he was a teenager. He described a vision where he saw his bedroom wall light up followed by a vision of a great revival taking place in stadiums. He described much of what I had seen in 1997, and shared the night before with Christy and Josiah. After he finished sharing this vision, he said he was going to speak about Samuel anointing David to be King. Christy and I were amazed, not only because this mirrored my experience from 1997, but it was as though our conversation from the night before was being replayed before us. You can't make this stuff up, but I have learned that this is simply how God rolls!

Since the prophetic ministry I received from Jeff Jansen on Valentine's Day in 2018, my experience from 1997 seemed to have been "unlocked" from my heart. The impartation from that night began to emerge with far more clarity for this very season we are in. I believe we are in the greatest moment of history for the Church, and I can hardly wait to see the emerging revival, reformation, and restoration increase on a global scale.

My prayer for you is this: That God's presence descends upon you and rises up within as you read this book. That the very Author and Finisher of our faith will descend upon you and emerge within you. That you will be consciously aware of our Lord as never before.

Revival can happen anywhere. I use the term "revival" because it is a common term that gives most all Christians a starting point for dialogue and thought. Whether you frame this move of God as an awakening, renewal, encounter, visitation, mass transformation, or perhaps something else entirely, one thing will be evident—the Refiner's fire will be sitting among us. Though I had a vision of stadiums, the emerging revival will certainly not be limited to stadiums. I believe we will see and hear of the fruit of revival far and wide. From stadiums to stables, tabernacles to tables, in cities, on farms, in prisons and barns. We will hear stories of the majesty and sovereignty of God from far and wide, personal and corporate accounts.

To be true, the most glorious moments I have had with the Lord was when I was alone. However, I do believe we will see a corporate manifestation that will be stunning. So prepare the way of the Lord, for suddenly the refining fire is surely coming to sit among us, and who can stand when He appears?

IT'S BIRTHING TIME

There is a baby being born, and I have good news: It's a new season and era. We get to be witnesses of these events. We are witnesses of the birth and the growth. We are also the carriers of that which is being born. It is a wonderful day to be a child of God!

I know some of you may be thinking, "What does this have to do with revival, reformation, and restoration?" Stay with me; we're going somewhere.

My wife, Christy, and I have nine children. (Yes, I know what causes it!) I have been there every time one of my children was born. However, I want to tell you the story of two of their deliveries. The first one I want to talk about occurred in 2001 when Destiny Hope came into the world. This was an interesting night that stands out differently from the births of our previous children.

It was a weekend night, and, when we arrived at the hospital, our doctor was not there. I am not sure if she was home or out with friends, but the nurses told us they were in touch with her. I could tell Christy was close to giving birth, as we have been through this a few times and I can see it in her eyes. I told the nurses this, but they insisted that the baby would not be born until the next day.

"No, this baby is closer than you think!" I argued back. Destiny was our fourth child, and I could simply see it on Christy's face. The contractions began getting more intense as the night wore on. Then, for whatever reason, the nurses came in and put a shot of morphine into Christy's IV line without asking us. Christy could feel it immediately and began to cry. She didn't ask for this, and knew they did it to slow down and control the birth of Destiny.

I was slightly angry, because I knew Destiny was ready to be born. While I'm sure there may have been a legitimate reason why they did this, I am convinced it was because the doctor didn't want to adjust her schedule for Destiny's birth. She wanted to control when the delivery would take place so it would suit her schedule.

Destiny didn't seem to care about this! It wasn't long before the nurses realized the morphine wasn't stopping the delivery, and they quickly called the doctor in. During the delivery process, there were some slight complications. Destiny's heartbeat would become extremely slow for a prolonged period of time during the contractions, which were not as intense as they should've been. I believe this was because of the medication the nurses gave Christy. (The morphine had caused her to feel very sick and nauseated, so they had given her medication for this as well.) I could see that the doctor was distressed as Destiny was born, and we are grateful her delivery took place without further issues.

The next delivery I want to tell you about took place in December of 2010. Mercy Grace, our eighth child, came into the world. Her delivery was shocking, to me at least.

We arrived at the hospital, this time in the middle of the night. Christy was determined to have this baby as close to natural as she could. They did hook her up to a monitoring device, but she was given no medication or epidural.

Once again, I could tell when she was close to delivering Mercy. "It's time. I can see it in her eyes and on her face," I told the nurses. Like before, they dismissed my remarks and told me they could monitor what was taking place from their station. A doctor was on call at that time, but it wasn't our doctor.

"This could take several hours," they told me.

I insisted that it wouldn't as the nurses left the room and Christy's contractions became more intense.

"She's coming!" Christy yelled.

The next thing I knew, here came Mercy Grace. She plopped right out in front of me. I thought I was going to fall over. No doctor, no nurses, just me and Christy! No hands touched her when she was born. The nurses came in immediately after Mercy came out. I remember the looks on their faces, and I am sure they remember the look on my face as well. I was furious that they had been so indifferent, but they were very humble and apologetic. The doctor would share their sentiment when he arrived later. They all knew they had dropped the ball. Nevertheless, Mercy Grace was born!

What does this have to do with revival and the things of God? I believe it has *everything* to do with these things. You see, everything in the Kingdom is born. To enter the Kingdom of God, we must be born again (John 3:1-3). We are birthed into the Kingdom.

You carry the hope of destiny within you, but destiny must be born. Men may come and try to slow it down for their own convenience, but destiny must be born. It's time! You carry mercy and grace as well, but mercy and grace must be born, and not by the hands of men. Unless the Lord builds the house, the house is built in vain.

REVIVAL IS BORN

Often, when the subject of revival comes up, we immediately think of names like *Finney, Spurgeon, Wesley, Campbell, Roberts, Edwards,* and others. We may also think of the more modern revivals of Azusa Street, Toronto, Brownsville, as well as others. While I love reading the accounts of these revivals, my approach in this book is to invite us to look through another lens. As great as these revivals were, they all had a starting point and an ending point, and I believe we are entering into a revival that shall have no end. As it was prophesied by many more recently, there have been prophetic words that go as far back as Smith Wigglesworth (1930s) that we are going to see a revival without ebb.

Revival by definition is *a restoration of consciousness, vigor, and strength; an awakening to the love, power, and purpose of God.* It could also be described as a move of God where His presence is manifested, quickening the masses or individuals who are experiencing His presence. I personally believe one absolute ingredient that separates true revival from "proclaimed revival" is the manifest presence of God. He Himself sits among us as a refiner's fire. I will speak more to this later.

So, how do we have it? How do we get there? Is it something we work our way to, or is it actually the discovery of what always was? Do we birth it, or does it birth us? Does it require sacrifice, or obedience? Does it require lots of prayer and fasting? (Most everyone who has studied revival would say "yes," but could it be that our perspective of these things may be shortsighted?)

I am not trying to take away from anyone's spiritual disciplines, but I am trying to take you into another possibility of thought. Consider this scripture, it is the account of Mary being told she would conceive a child, and it further speaks of Elizabeth also carrying a child in her old age, which we now know was John the Baptist. The forerunner and the revival for all mankind in the wombs of two relatives. Imagine this for just a moment. It is not only the literal event that took place, but the prophetic picture of things to come.

Then the angel said to her, "Do not be afraid, Mary, for you have found favor with God. And behold, you will conceive in your womb and bring forth a Son, and shall call His name Jesus. He will be great, and will be called the Son of the Highest; and the Lord God will give Him the throne of His father David. And He will reign over the house of Jacob forever, and of His kingdom there will be no end."

Then Mary said to the angel, "How can this be, since I do not know a man?"

> And the angel answered and said to her, "The Holy Spirit will come upon you, and the power of the Highest will overshadow you; therefore, also, that Holy One who is to be born will be called the Son of God. Now indeed, Elizabeth your relative has also conceived a son in her old age; and this is now the sixth month for her who was called barren. ~ Luke 1:30-36

The forerunner and the Christ child carried in their mothers' wombs through the promise of God. I will speak more about this later in the book, but in this moment, the forerunner and the promised revival are carried in the wombs of the hearts of sons and daughters. This has already started, but the increase is going to be obvious. The birthing is about to be seen like it has never been seen before. It is the days we are living in. It's time!

Revival is conceived in the hearts of believers through the hearing of faith. It's an immaculate conception carried in our spiritual wombs until we give birth to that which was conceived. The very promises of God are conceived in our hearts and birthed into the earth.

> "For this reason a man shall leave his father and mother and be joined to his wife, and the two shall become one flesh." This is a great mystery, but I speak concerning Christ and the church. ~ Ephesians 5:31-32

We are the bride of Christ. Through the union of marriage, there is a mystery to be revealed about our relationship as believers with the Bridegroom.

As a father of nine children, it was through the union between my wife and I where conception occurred, and my wife carried the living promise of life within her—little lives God knew even before they were in her womb. Yes, I carried the seed, and she carried the egg, but what transpired in conception is the mystery of life. A life that came from God, which He knew before He sent them to earth (Jeremiah 1:5). A life that carries the promise of revival and purpose. An earthen vessel designed to carry and demonstrate the Kingdom from which they came. When is the last time you looked at someone with these thoughts in mind?

Through our passion-filled pursuit and experience of God's presence, our hearts lay bare before the Lord, and His seed is spoken into our hearts and His promise is conceived in us as we literally carry the miracle of life within our hearts, until the appropriate time when what we carry can be birthed into the earth. However, "I'm not making it; it is making me" as the old Rich Mullins song states. "It's the very truth of God and not the invention of any man." That thought was penned to music in Rich's song, *Creed*, which is a great description of what I am speaking of.

I think we sometimes have misconceptions of revival as well. I have often thought that when revival comes, everything will be perfect. However, I recognize that this depends on what our definition of "perfect" is. While I would never take away from what revival could be, I don't want to have an assumed view of how revival will always look, either. Revival could look like when Paul was struck blind through his visitation with Jesus on the road to Damascus. He went into the experience one way and came out another. This created such a profound change in one moment. Paul became an entirely different being—a man on fire, a man who endured shipwreck, a man who was bitten by a venomous snake and simply shook it off, a man who suffered at the hands of evil men, a man who was beaten several times and left for dead. In his own words, there were times when he "despaired of life itself" (2 Corinthians 1:8). He even wrote most of the scripture we read while he was chained to a Roman Soldier under house arrest. It took extraordinary revival at work within his heart to write about the freedom and grace of Christ while in chains.

Perhaps revival was speaking to us when Jesus was literally dying on the cross but still found Himself able to say, "Forgive them, Father, they don't know what they are doing" (Luke 23:34). What kind of power can do such things?

I believe we see revival as something we are working *toward* rather than working *from*. Our efforts should be from where we are seated, with Christ in "heavenly places" (Ephesians 2:6). Perhaps our works are more about working *through* something than working *to* something. Perhaps we are discovering and growing up in that which was there from the beginning. Discovery sparks our imagination and the faith of a child grasps what cannot be taught by the wisdom of men. When we become as children (Matthew 18:3), hope arises and our longings fulfilled become a tree of life (Proverbs 13:12).

In the story of Rachel, which begins in Genesis 29, Rachel couldn't bear children for Jacob and she cried out to God saying, "Give me children, or I'll die!" (Genesis 30:1). Her womb was barren. It was the longing of her heart to bear a child, and her heart was sick. The Lord heard her prayers, and she conceived as she desired.

We should pray for God to increase our hunger and desire for the things of God with the desperation of Rachel, yet, we should believe He is a good God, knowing that He answers those prayers.

BIRTHING THESE THINGS OF THE SPIRIT

I'm going to speak with authority about a mystery that I know little about. It's the revelation of being the bride of Christ, because though we are physical sons and daughters, we are all indeed the bride of Christ as well. Where sons speak of the inheritance and authority of their Father's house, the bride speaks of what is birthed through intimacy in the secret place with the King.

Christy and I have had nine children, and we have also lost nine children. As many as we have had, we have lost. I was present at every event. I have left sobbing, and I have left rejoicing. You can call us fools if you want to, but when we carry something, we will not abandon it. We never quit believing for God's goodness over us, and He has come through time and time again!

There is a difference between trying to "push through" a promise we catch a glimpse of and "pressing into" the grace of the promise through faith. The promise is achieved by grace through faith (Romans 4:16), which enables us to enter into His rest (Hebrews 4:1). Everything from the Kingdom comes by grace through faith, just as our salvation did (Ephesians 2:8). Rest is the fruit of faith and grace at work in our lives. In fact, in the natural, if you have problems early on in a pregnancy, your doctor will order you to rest rather than exert more effort!

When you have the revelation that you are the bride of Christ, you can very well expect to carry something in your spiritual womb. If this hasn't happened to you yet, it is coming. In fact, if you have been born of God, you already carry a lot more than you may realize. Yet, in this narrative, I am specifically speaking of a promise God gives you for a specific purpose. God sows His word of promise into us, and we carry it for an appointed time. If you push at the wrong time, you'll either kill your baby, yourself or it will be born pre-mature. In either case, suffering and sometimes death will be the fruit of your actions. What baby am I speaking of? The vision, the promise of the Lord that is spoken to you.

There is a time to rest, and this, for the most part, reveals our level of faith far more than our pushing does. There is certainly a time to push, which is a minute moment of the process. When Christy goes into labor, she endures the contractions but she doesn't push. Her body, by nature, is preparing itself to deliver, and the intense contractions are a way of preparation for delivery. She will not be asked by a doctor to push until that very moment comes, and the push is the shortest part of the entire process.

The evil "wisdom of this age" has told us that we must always push our way to and through everything. That's what the world does, and we are called to something different. Yes, we do play a part of the process. We pray, we sow, we water, but God gives the increase (1 Corinthians 3:6). Jesus is the Author and Finisher of our faith (Hebrews 12:2); it is not dependent upon our ability to push.

> If I have told you earthly things and you do not believe, how will you believe if I tell you heavenly things? ~ John 3:12

> Pains as of a woman in childbirth come to him, but he is a child without wisdom; when the time arrives, he doesn't have the sense to come out of the womb. ~ Hosea 13:13, NIV.

Jesus said that when we see nations turning on each other with earthquakes, famines and the like, that these were the beginning of birth pangs (Matthew 24:7-8). I would say that we are living in the times of birth pangs. In the natural, we refer to them as "contractions." The whole earth is experiencing contractions, because there are things that are being born and more things to come.

We are entering into a time where things that have been carried in the Spirit are going to be birthed into this world. Rest until you "know that you know" that it is time to push. How can you know this? By keeping your eyes on Jesus, and committing yourself to hear His voice above all others. We were never meant to prosper apart from Him. Unless the Spirit of the Lord builds the house, the house is built in vain (Psalm 127:1). Trust your "midwife," Jesus, the Author and Finisher of your faith. Knowing *how* to push is a good thing, but the wisdom of knowing *when* to push is far more profitable.

Some of the greatest gifts of God that have been birthed in the earth were birthed through the most unlikely people. Some even appeared to be illegitimate at first. That, my friends, is the wonderful mystery of a kind and loving God.

You may still ask, "What's this got to do with revival?"

I would say, "Everything!" which will hopefully be discovered as you continue to read.

THERE ARE TWO HOUSES IN OUR GARDEN

There were two trees in the garden, the tree of life and the tree of the knowledge of good and evil. One produced life, the other produced death. Adam and Eve were told to not eat from the tree of the knowledge of good and evil, because if they did, they would surely die (Genesis 2:17). Most of us are familiar with this story.

Today, for those of us who are born of God through Christ, we will eventually see that there are two houses being built. One is being built by the Lord—the other is built in vain. Both have their apostles, prophets, evangelists, pastors, teachers, followers, watchmen, deacons, intercessors, administrators, food banks, and fundraisers. Yet one is built by the Lord, and the other is built in vain.

Both of them pray and use Scripture; declare what they believe is holy and true, and believe they hold the answer the whole world needs. Yet, one is built by the Lord, and the other is built in vain. One reveals Christ, the other has a form of Godliness but denies the power thereof (2 Timothy 3:5).

> Unless the Lord builds the house, They labor in vain who build it; Unless the Lord guards the city, The watchman stays awake in vain. ~ Psalm 127:1

What does it mean when something is "built in vain?"
Let's look at a definition:

Vain

1. *excessively proud of or concerned about one's own appearance, qualities, achievements, etc.; conceited: a vain dandy.*
2. *proceeding from or showing pride in or concern about one's appearance, qualities, etc.; resulting from or displaying vanity: He made some vain remarks about his accomplishments.*
3. *ineffectual or unsuccessful; futile: vain hopes; a vain effort; a vain war.*
4. *without real significance, value, or importance; baseless or worthless: vain pageantry; vain display.*
5. *Archaic. senseless or foolish.*

Source: Dictionary.com

I love an excellent presentation as good as anyone. However, I realize that presentation without substance will fail us. If I have to choose between a fantastic presentation empty of His presence and a poor presentation where the Spirit of the Lord is, I'll take the latter every time.

Abraham was promised that his descendants would be as the number of stars in the heavens and the sands of the seashore (Genesis 22:17). That's immeasurable by man's abilities. Abraham's wife, Sarah, could not conceive a child at this point. Therefore, she convinced Abraham to take her servant, Hagar, so that he would have a descendant.

The Lord had already promised Abraham he would have descendants, and Sarah was his wife, but they ended up trying to fulfill the promise of God with their own reasoning. Abraham did have a son though Hagar, who was named Ishmael.

Later, when Sarah conceived, she gave birth to her son, Isaac. Abraham now had two sons. One was the son promised by the Lord; the other was the son of his own reasoning. They have been at enmity ever since. (In fact, the roots of Christianity and Islam can be traced to Isaac and Ishmael, respectively.)

This is a prophetic picture of the difference between the Lord building a house and a house that is built in vain. There are many who are still trying to build and fulfill God's promise using their own reasoning and conclusions today.

I would say that every person born again has been seduced by the enemy to eat from the tree of the knowledge of good and evil at one time or another. That's why repentance is a necessary part of our lives, why we confess our sins and return to the superior reality of the eternal life in Christ. If we need revival, it is because we no longer see from the perspective of our first love as we did when we were initially born again.

If every man as an individual can be seduced into the fallen reasoning that comes from the forbidden tree, then every local assembly can collectively do the same, as many have. When this happens, revival and restoration become necessary.

That which is built by the Spirit of the Lord must be sustained by the Spirit of the Lord as well. We must not only be filled with the Spirit, but be continually infilled with the Spirit. We are a house individually, corporately, and globally. As individuals, we are being built but the Lord. However, we sometimes build things in our personal lives that have nothing in common with who Jesus designed us to be.

It is also possible for us to follow someone who is following after the Spirit of God, while remaining unaware of what spirit we ourselves are of.

> And when His disciples James and John saw this, they said, "Lord, do You want us to command fire to come down from heaven and consume them, just as Elijah did?" But He turned and rebuked them, and said, "You do not know what manner of spirit you are of. ~ Luke 9:54-55

Yikes! Jesus could not have rebuked them if they had not been following Him. He didn't do this to condemn them, but to teach them something.

Unless the Lord builds the house, the house is built in vain. Unless the Lord writes this book, this book is written in vain. Yet, unless I put my fingerprints on it, it will not be written. My point is, no matter what it is we do, if it is not through a heart of love that comes through the inspiration of the Lord Himself, it is all vanity of vanities.

We hold what Paul wrote to be canon. Yet, Paul Himself said he had not arrived. How is it possible for a man who had not arrived to write Scripture? Isn't that the great mystery and miracle of it all, that God could turn one of the Church's greatest persecutors and murderers into an apostle? Did God not also turn fishermen into apostles of the Lamb?

To be a builder in the house the Lord is building, we must first *be* a house that the Lord is building.

REVIVAL AND THE RESTORATION OF ALL THINGS

On June 1, 2010, I awoke at 3:00am to the realization that the presence of the Lord was filling my bedroom. It was not a visitation in the sense that I saw the Lord with my natural eyes, but a visitation where I knew that I knew He was present, and would have instructions for me. This was a time where I was going through an intense personal crisis. Just three years prior, I had lost our home, our vehicles, our money, and our credit. I had to file bankruptcy, and my health started declining in several areas simultaneously. I suffered with depression, anxiety, extreme guilt and shame for all the loss we endured. I had begun to drink heavily in an attempt to medicate myself from the intense pain and pressure I was under. I felt like and experienced the reality of being an abandoned wreck. Nevertheless, this night, God was present, and I knew He was going to speak to me.

I got into our old van and drove out into the woods so I could be alone with God. As soon as I turned off the pavement, the Lord spoke to me.

I'm not mad at you.

In that moment, I didn't just hear His words; I felt as if He was holding me in His arms. I could feel the sincerity of His words. They were true, and they penetrated every fiber of my being. I wept profusely, sobbing with tears and brokenness. I could not wrap my brain around this moment, nor could I refuse it. How could He not be angry with me after all of my failures? Yet, as I was experiencing this moment, I could sense years of accumulated "poison" leaving me as His Spirit seemed to replace all of the pain and anguish I felt with faith, hope, and love. It was the oil of His Spirit pouring in and the poison of this world flowing out.

About thirty minutes later, He said this to me, *Men get a glimpse of what I want to do in the earth, and then they try to build it with their hands.*

After He said this, I experienced wave after wave of His presence pouring over me. Each time it happened, I knew this word He just spoke was being imparted to me. I felt an extraordinary understanding of something I knew I could not fully articulate. I was also still weeping from the first thing He said to me.

Thirty minutes later, God spoke to me a final time: *Contend for My presence.*

As with the other statements, waves of His presence swept over me.

For the last eight years, this experience has brought extraordinary change to my life and sense of perception. It was given to me for the foundational purpose of how I would articulate future revelation I would hear. It was a deeper change to my perspective of who God is as well.

These things He spoke to me will be revisited a few times as we journey through the pages. The first being, *I'm not mad at you.* Before we speak of revival, reformation, and restoration, this first word must be established in our hearts. Who could follow anyone who was in constant anger toward them? Imagine if you were a kid, and all you saw was your parents' anger toward you. You would believe you could never do anything right in their eyes, and you would feel as if you were in a prison. The same is true in the workplace. If your employer stayed in perpetual anger toward you, you would despise your job, and your employer as well.

We must learn to see God as a Good Father. His love for you and your true value is directly reflected in the price He was willing to pay to have you. That price was His only Son. This should also speak of the Son's love for His Father, and for you as well. Before we venture into the wonderful promises of God, we must be clear that He is indeed wonderful, and that His thoughts toward us are always for our *good*. He is a good, good Father, and I am privileged to follow Him and share what He has shown me.

The second thing the Lord spoke to me was, *Men get a glimpse of what I want to do in the earth, and then they try to build it with their hands.*

This speaks of folks getting a glimpse of truth, whether in vision or word, then attempting to build or plant what they saw in the earth using their own reasoning and effort. It doesn't mean that the original word or idea wasn't from God, but what begun by His Spirit soon became a work of the flesh. This can happen even with good things, such as planting a church or starting a ministry. God gives someone a vision, but the person then attempts to make it happen in their own strength and leaves God out of the process or greatly limits His involvement. We do this when we create our own plans and then take them to God right before we execute them for His stamp of approval, rather than seeking to understand His methods to accomplish His vision.

The third word the Lord spoke to me was, *Contend for My presence.*

Contending for the presence of God means we purposely keep our hearts and minds turned toward Him as we go about our days. The only thing that has ever changed anyone is an encounter with the presence of Christ Jesus. Colossians speaks of this great exchange that occurred when we met Christ for the first time, and this will continue to occur by the Lord's design.

> If then you were raised with Christ, seek those things which are above, where Christ is, sitting at the right hand of God. Set your mind on things above, not on things on the earth. For you died, and your life is hidden with Christ in God. When Christ who is our life appears, then you also will appear with Him in glory. ~ Colossians 3:1-4

People get glimpses of what God wants to do, but it must be God who builds it, or it's built in vain. While we are watchmen on the wall (Psalm 127:1) who steward the mysteries of God (1 Corinthians

4:1), unless He watches over that which He has built, those who stand guard do so in vain. Our part as those who have a glimpse of what He is doing is to do what we see Him do and say what we hear Him say. Our part is to live by every word that proceeds from the mouth of God, to testify of what we have seen and heard. This doesn't mean we don't have an active role to play; it just means that God is in charge, not us. To get the idea of what this will look like, we have to look at how the first revival and reformation of the Church began shortly after Jesus' resurrection.

> And He opened their understanding, that they might comprehend the Scriptures.
> Then He said to them, "Thus it is written, and thus it was necessary for the Christ to suffer and to rise from the dead the third day, and that repentance and remission of sins should be preached in His name to all nations, beginning at Jerusalem. And you are witnesses of these things. Behold, I send the Promise of My Father upon you; but tarry in the city of Jerusalem until you are endued with power from on high." ~ Luke 24:45-49

In this moment, Jesus is telling His disciples that they are witnesses of the things of God. He then tells them to go to Jerusalem and remain there until they are clothed with power from on high. What was it they were waiting for? We know from Scripture that it was the Holy Spirit, but what did they know at the time? Did they know exactly what it would look like? Could they articulate what they were going to witness before it happened? I would say, no way. They went to Jerusalem at the Lord's instruction and waited for something promised but not understood.

Imagine, if you will, waiting on something that the Lord promised, a sovereign move and empowerment of God. Everyone was devoted to praying while they were waiting. Yet, all they knew is they were waiting for something and, somehow, they would know when it happened.

Could you build this moment that Jesus spoke of? No; you wouldn't know where to begin. You would only know what Jesus had said, nothing more. Listen to the description of the event in Scripture:

> And suddenly there came a sound from heaven, as of a rushing mighty wind, and it filled the whole house where they were sitting. Then there appeared to them divided tongues, as of fire, and one sat upon each of them. And they were all filled with the Holy Spirit and began to speak with other tongues, as the Spirit gave them utterance. ~ Acts 2:2-4

Oh, what this must have felt like when it finally happened! The twelve who walked with Jesus had no significant order or set of instructions going into this moment, but order began to shape and form when they came out of this moment.

We have heard it said by many that *glory follows order*, but I am fully convinced it's actually the other way around, that *order follows glory*. We do what we know to do and we say what we know to say; however, order is discovered when God's presence is manifested. Revival is not discovered through the order of men, otherwise, who would we ultimately believe is building the house? Unless the Spirit builds the house, the house is built in vain. Unless the Lord stewards and guards the house, the house will function in vain. The glory is not discovered through five-fold ministry. Five-fold ministry is discovered through the glory of God, and men are witnesses to what they have seen, heard, and been clothed with from on high. To be a witness of things, we must witness something from seeing and hearing that which comes from God. It is at this point the glory is revealed through men. At this point, those functioning in different offices of ministry will reveal that which they have witnessed.

> That which was from the beginning, which we have heard, which we have seen with our eyes, which we have looked upon, and our hands have handled, concerning the Word of life—the life was manifested, and we have seen, and bear witness, and declare to

you that eternal life which was with the Father and was manifested to us—that which we have seen and heard we declare to you, that you also may have fellowship with us; and truly our fellowship is with the Father and with His Son Jesus Christ. ~ 1 John 1:1-3

When a group believes that revival will come through the order they have established, they will more than likely find themselves taking some sort of credit for it. However, that which is built by the Spirit will come through the Spirit, often suddenly. Will people participate and play a role in what is built by the Spirit? Absolutely they will, and they will know it is the Spirit who is building the house. To God be the glory forever and ever! Amen.

AN ENEMY OF REVIVAL

The spirit of religion emerges when people use their own reasoning to build finite parameters or limits while attempting to express and reveal an infinite God, and then worship their parameters. Another way to say this is that people instinctively create a box they believe can explain the mystery of God, then worship their box. The enemy tries to trap us into drawing our own conclusions about God and then building on our own human reasoning. This leads to us creating and worshiping a God we are comfortable with, but when you get down to it, we are really worshiping our own reasoning. This is something we should all have a healthy concern about.

We do this with individuals as well. Five-fold ministry has been and is being restored back to the body of Christ, and accepted by some as sound doctrine. Yet, everyone who is introduced to this revelation has their own boxes as to how those who are called by God will walk in their gifting. Much of what I hear and read appears to be shortsighted by human reasoning.

We believe we clearly know what an apostle is. We believe we clearly know what a prophet is and what they do. We clearly believe the same concerning evangelists, pastors, and teachers. Even some of those gifted to walk in the grace of one of these offices seem shortsighted concerning these things. To be honest we are all shortsighted concerning the things of God, but that's why we need Jesus, is it not? That is why we must contend for His presence. All we truly know is what we have seen and heard, and we testify to that. We go too far when we reach conclusions about things we know little to nothing about. When we do this, we have created another box we will worship.

No matter what our revelation is, whether it be concerning five-fold ministry, prayer movements, or denominations, they will all become tombs full of dead men's bones if we turn a fluid move into an unmovable and limited box. They become monuments of what once was, instead of the living, moving, life-giving, life-changing and fluid Church of the living God.

> However, we speak wisdom among those who are mature, yet not the wisdom of this age, nor of the rulers of this age, who are coming to nothing. But we speak the wisdom of God in a mystery, the hidden wisdom which God ordained before the ages for our glory, which none of the rulers of this age knew; for had they known, they would not have crucified the Lord of glory.
> But as it is written:
> "Eye has not seen, nor ear heard,
> Nor have entered into the heart of man
> The things which God has prepared for those who love Him."
> But God has revealed them to us through His Spirit. For the Spirit searches all things, yes, the deep things of God. For what man knows the things of a man except the spirit of the man which is in him? Even so no one knows the things of God except the Spirit of God. Now we have received, not the spirit of the world, but the Spirit who is from God, that we might know the things that have been freely given to us by God.
> These things we also speak, not in words which man's wisdom teaches but which the Holy Spirit teaches, comparing spiritual things with spiritual. ~ 1 Corinthians 2:6-13

This Scripture speaks to what we are talking about. I have read several accounts of the revivals and reformations of the past, and found that while they hold keys and identifying markers, they do not fully reveal what the impending revival will look like in its fullness. Thus, it is important that we begin with a level footing in order to hear God's heart for what this should look like. This may require some humility, especially toward other believers and worship styles that are outside of our current proverbial boxes.

Am I an authority on this topic? No! The Lord is my authority. Many folks have seen many things concerning revival and reformation—in part. The whole point of everything I have said to this point is that while we may know some things, see some things, and experience some things, we must also recognize that we don't know everything about what we might see before we see it play out in front of us.

> Eye has not seen, nor ear heard, nor have entered into the heart of man the things which God has prepared for those who love Him. ~ 1 Corinthians 2:9

We must remove presumption from the table when talking about the Lord's purposes, understanding that everything hinges on the work of the Spirit and we must remain dependent on Him. The revelation of our everlasting Lord is ever-increasing on the earth, even as you read this sentence.

REVIVAL, REFORMATION, RESTORATION, AND THE ELIJAH COMMISSION

As I mentioned earlier, Mary was carrying the promise of the Christ child while Elizabeth was carrying the spirit of Elijah—John the Baptist. I find it so interesting that it was six months prior to Mary's conception. This paints a prophetic picture as well.

> And His disciples asked Him, saying, "Why then do the scribes say that Elijah must come first?"
> Jesus answered and said to them, "Indeed, Elijah is coming first and will restore all things." ~ Matthew 17:10-11

In this passage of Scripture, Jesus says Elijah will come and restore all things. At the moment in time when He said this, John the Baptist had already been beheaded; however, Jesus referred to him as one who walked in the spirit of Elijah. So, there is both the reference of the Spirit of Elijah in the life of John the Baptist, as well as a future reference.

> "Behold, I send My messenger, and he will prepare the way before Me. And the Lord, whom you seek, will suddenly come to His temple, Even the Messenger of the covenant, In whom you delight. Behold, He is coming," Says the Lord of hosts. ~ Malachi 3:1

REVIVAL, REFORMATION, RESTORATION, AND THE ELIJAH COMMISSION

This literally happened on the day of Pentecost and is a prophetic description of the "latter rain that will be greater than the former rain," which is also articulated in Scripture (John 2:23, Haggai 2:9). If Pentecost was the catalyst for forming the Church, I believe this same type of move will be the catalyst that reforms and restores the Church as well.

> "Behold, I will send you Elijah the prophet Before the coming of the great and dreadful day of the Lord. And he will turn the hearts of the fathers to the children, And the hearts of the children to their fathers, Lest I come and strike the earth with a curse." ~ Malachi 4:5-6

We know the "dreadful day of the Lord" has not come yet. This passage speaks of the Elijah commission as a future reality, and they point to the function of those called to carry this mantle of authority in the Church presently. To be commissioned is to be sent.

This is a profound Scripture to me. It holds a great deal of mystery and speaks of the honor and responsibility God placed on John the Baptist.

> For I say to you, among those born of women there is not a greater prophet than John the Baptist; but he who is least in the kingdom of God is greater than he."
>
> And when all the people heard Him, even the tax collectors justified God, having been baptized with the baptism of John. But the Pharisees and lawyers rejected the will of God for themselves, not having been baptized by him. ~ Luke 7:28-30

Wait a minute—according to this Scripture, everyone who heard Jesus' words, even the sinners, acknowledged God's way was right, with the exception of those who had not yet been baptized by John. It says the Pharisees and the experts in the Law rejected the purposes of God because, apparently, they rejected John's baptism. Whoa! So, according to Scripture, Elijah is coming and will either be received or rejected. Eternity weighs in the balance for many. The blessing upon the earth is at risk if the Elijah's of God do not rise up. That's quite a task, both to them who walk in this mantle and those who hear them. As Leonard Ravenhill once said, "Where are the Elijah's of God?"

Where are the Elijah's of God? Where do they come from? Where are they born? They will be sent by the will of God, not the will of men, though men and women should recognize and receive them. These Elijah's will prepare the way before Jesus returns so people will recognize and hear the Spirit of God when He speaks.

When is this prophet born? On the day of conception? Hardly. For his idea was born long before, in the heart of an ancient God, ages before he was in his mother's womb. He was formed by the hands of Another's intentions before he ever saw the light of the world he lives in. He was sent to be a contradiction of rational thought—an anomaly. A mystery to some, a fool to others; a comfort to some, yet an affliction for many to endure. At times, He speaks with the passion of our relentless Lord; at other times, He speaks gently, as a loving Father. He often appears to be a living, breathing contradiction to what some hold sacred, but he carries a message of uncompromised devotion.

Why does God need one such as this? Who else would be His fool to this world? He is no fool in the eyes of his Maker; yet, he is often born into a pit or soon finds one, for it is in this proverbial pit where he receives his training. It is in this place that he has the time required to come to terms with the fact that he is foolish in every way to this world, and accepts the proper conclusions about himself. It is also in this place that he learns to hear the voice of One that he couldn't hear as clearly before—the voice of One crying in the wilderness. It is here that he discovers the precious life that he will draw his strength from for the rest of his physical life. This revelation does not come from pomp and circumstance, only the pit. It does not come from being esteemed by men, but from prolonged seasons of brokenness and loneliness. In this, the prophet learns to stand, even if he has to stand alone.

REVIVAL, REFORMATION, RESTORATION, AND THE ELIJAH COMMISSION

Why is this necessary? The answer to this question will not be fully known until one crosses over that which separates them from their purpose. Even then, they see as though through a dim glass (1 Corinthians 13:12). God does not allow things to happen any other way. We long for freedom, but it does not come in the way we imagine. Not everyone makes it through the process, but those who do will be changed into that which was from the beginning.

This prophetic voice will tear down the high places built by the elitism of men and raise up the lowly. They will make crooked paths straight and level, so those behind can run freely. This is what it means to be a *forerunner*. They are charged to challenge and bring down the elitism and pride of men while lifting up the humble in heart, the broken, and the downtrodden. They will expose elitism, hypocrisy, and the corruption of the evil wisdom of this age for what it is. This burns within their heart. Their fight is not with flesh and blood, but against the principalities, powers of darkness, and wickedness in high places that corrupts the hearts of men.

They will arrest and deliver our hearts with a conviction that will enable us to see and hear God. They will root out that which comes to destroy, pulling down our vain imaginations and ideologies that exalts themselves above the very truth and heart of God. Their very presence destroys the works of the devil, because the spirit of Elijah is the Spirit of the Lord given for a specific purpose. They will throw down any evil that imposes itself to do harm, and route the false ones who made the god they worship an "ism" of their own reasoning.

They will restore all things to a place of wholeness, both individually and corporately, turning the hearts of the fathers to their children, and the hearts of the children to their fathers. If this doesn't happen, the land will be stricken with total destruction (Malachi 4:6).

Their knees only bow to the One who sent them, because they answer to no one but the One who sent them. Yet, they will bow their knees when the One who sent them speaks through a mere child. They will not compromise their message because they know only one house is built by the Lord, and the other is built in vain. They will not compromise or bow their knee to that which is built in vain, or its apostles and prophets.

What is their reward for such a thing? To hear and know the Father's voice. To speak that in which they were given. To do the will of the One who sent them.

What is their message? *Prepare the way of the Lord by responding to what the Father is saying and doing.* They point to Christ above all as the One whose very word holds all of creation in place. This mission consumes them, and it in itself is the reward.

The Elijah commission is a prophetic mantle for a specific purpose that will rest on those who are called to walk in it and choose to say "yes" to this call. I have spoken about the prophets who will walk in this commission. However, in Rick Joyner's book *The Call*, He said that some apostles will have this forerunner mantle operating in their ministry as well, who are sent out ahead of the others for the purpose of preparing the way of the Lord. I believe this is true. I have met those called to be apostles who carry this Elijah mantle as powerful as I have ever seen on anyone.

I have a friend who is a prophet and evangelist who carries the Elijah mantle. I refer to him as both a prophet and an evangelist because I honestly see both at work in his life in equal measure. Folks like him challenge our assumptions and our boxes. While the Elijah mantle is normally associated with the prophetic, God can do what He wants with who He wants.

When God sends an equipper, He equips all who receive with the reward of the equipper. Concerning this reward, increase is always set before us when we receive any ministry gift in the name of the ministry gift. As Scripture indicates, if you receive a prophet in the name of a prophet, then you receive the prophet's reward (Matthew 10:41). The prophet's reward reveals the heart of God in a matter. Wisdom, insight, and power have always been associated with the prophetic reward. Elisha, who walked in a double portion or Elijah's mantle, brought wealth to the Shunammite woman because she made a room for him in her house, knowing it would bring blessing to her family (2 Kings 4:8-37). I will go further to say that the more we receive him who was sent, the greater the blessings there will be upon the Body as a whole.

THE CIRCUMCISION

I am going to assume we all know what circumcision means in both a literal and spiritual sense. While in the natural this is the cutting away of foreskin, in the Spirit this is a metaphorical type and shadow of a spiritual event that is done in the hearts of believers. In the Old Testament, circumcision was a literal requirement that took place among men who were in covenant with God. This act would normally take place when the male was younger; however, there were accounts when it was done to older men. This couldn't have been fun to endure. While the act was a literal command to those who were in covenant with God, it was a type and shadow of what takes place in the hearts of men (and women) who are being transformed into the likeness of Christ. In Christ, true circumcision is of the heart.

> For we are the circumcision, who worship God in the Spirit, rejoice in Christ Jesus, and have no confidence in the flesh, though I also might have confidence in the flesh. ~ Philippians 3:3

> For he is not a Jew who is one outwardly, nor is circumcision that which is outward in the flesh; but he is a Jew who is one inwardly; and circumcision is that of the heart, in the Spirit, not in the letter; whose praise is not from men but from God. ~ Romans 2:28-29

> Brothers and sisters, if I am still preaching circumcision, why am I still being persecuted? In that case the offense of the cross has

been abolished. As for those agitators, I wish they would go the whole way and emasculate themselves! ~ Galatians 5:11-12, NIV

The Spirit of God is alive on the inside of us. He is shaping and molding us into the image of Christ. When ministers properly function in their calling, rightly dividing the word of truth, our hearts are in effect being circumcised by the hearing of the word. It is the separating of the precious from the vile. It is the process that removes the useless while protecting a son or daughter's ability to reproduce, spiritually speaking. There is a difference between one who attempts to bring about reform through castration and one who brings circumcision for the purpose of transformation. When a minister has wrong motives corrupting their message, they will often emasculate the authority of the individuals they were supposed to liberate and commission.

I am speaking metaphorically, yet literally in a spiritual sense. However, to the one experiencing either, it could outwardly look and feel the same without the Holy Spirit. If you are a Christian, by faith in the finished work of Christ, your heart has been "circumcised." However, through our life experience, that which has occurred by faith is happening through transitional life experience in our walk with Christ. Receiving the ministry of others is part of that process. As Paul said we were *'built'* on the foundation of the apostles and prophets, and we are *'being built'* together (Ephesians 2:19-22).

We know that circumcision removes that which is useless, but what is it that is being removed? The obvious answer is our sinful nature, but what else could be removed? How about the stronghold that human reasoning has on our hearts? I am reminded of the scripture, "Trust in the Lord with all your hearts, and do not lean on your own understanding" (Proverbs 3:5). It is through our own reasoning that doubt, unbelief, fear, worry, strife, and the like are born. In fact, it is through our own reasoning that *every* evil is born. Of course, there are times when it is okay to rely on human reasoning, and even times when it can be used as a tool for good. However, this ends when our own reasoning attempts to assert itself over the word of the Lord. Our own reasoning knows nothing of

THE CIRCUMCISION

the things of God, because that which comes by the Spirit is discerned by the spirit within us, the part of us that is a new creation.

> For the message of the cross is foolishness to those who are perishing, but to us who are being saved it is the power of God. For it is written: "I will destroy the wisdom of the wise, and bring to nothing the understanding of the prudent." ~ 1 Corinthians 1:18-19

> Because the foolishness of God is wiser than men, and the weakness of God is stronger than men. ~ 1 Corinthians 1:25

> These things we also speak, not in words which man's wisdom teaches but which the Holy Spirit teaches, comparing spiritual things with spiritual. But the natural man does not receive the things of the Spirit of God, for they are foolishness to him; nor can he know them, because they are spiritually discerned.
> ~ 1 Corinthians 2:13-14

One aspect of corporate prophetic ministry is bringing circumcision to the hearts of those who are "being built" together. Does this bring division? Yes, it does. It separates the precious from the vile so that we can transition into the fullness that God created us for. I am not speaking of people themselves as either precious or vile; rather, I am speaking of mindsets we have. This is not an attempt to separate "true believers" from others; it is laying the ax to the root of the tree of the knowledge of good and evil and establishing our hearts in the tree of life. Only when the word is rejected are people physically separated from other people.

Moses was commanded by the Lord to circumcise his son. He overlooked this command, a mistake that nearly cost him his life. His wife Zipporah witnesses this and circumcised her son, touching Moses' feet with his foreskin. (Exodus 4:24-26). This sounds a bit radical, does it not?

Prophets reveal circumcision, while Jezebel comes to castrate the sons and make herself trophies of that which she removed. Both are spiritually bloody, yet the prophet reveals covenant and Jezebel reveals a murderous coup. Prophets cut off that which the useless, while Jezebel renders the sons useless. Prophets turn sons into forerunners, Jezebel turns sons into submissive eunuchs through demonic manipulation and intimidation as she disguises herself as an angel of light. God called us to be His sons and daughters, His bride who will birth the promise of who He is into the earth. Jezebel seeks to destroy this work by any means possible.

> "I am the vine, you are the branches. He who abides in Me, and I in him, bears much fruit; for without Me you can do nothing. If anyone does not abide in Me, he is cast out as a branch and is withered; and they gather them and throw them into the fire, and they are burned." ~ John 15:5-6

In these days of grace, we have time and opportunity to be grafted into the Vine and produce fruit. Thank God for His grace as we mature! His pruning is always for our good, and it always brings unity to those whose hearts are turned toward Him.

As sure as a great awakening is coming, I see a great divine confrontation and circumcision coming upon the hearts of those who follow Jesus, on a global level, as well. This is necessary, because an evil wisdom of this age called elitism has blinded our hearts.

First and foremost, elitism is fully rooted in pride. It is the manifestation of pride. It can take the form of racial supremacy, intellectual supremacy, financial supremacy, artistic supremacy, political supremacy, denominational supremacy, and even spiritual supremacy. It is not limited to any of these things. While we point fingers at what type of supremacy is being advocated, what the elitism represents isn't as important as the fact that elitism is the driving force behind it. Elitism has proven itself over and over to be a spiritual killer. Elitism decides which forms of supremacy are acceptable and which forms aren't. To even possess this kind of mindset is intellectual and spiritual insanity. Elitism is the epitome of hypocrisy.

THE CIRCUMCISION

Elitism is why Lucifer was kicked out of Heaven. Scripture declares that he looked at himself and was well pleased. "Your heart became proud on account of your beauty, and you corrupted your wisdom because of your splendor" (Ezekiel 28:17).

Never build a reputation for yourself that you cannot afford to lose for the sake of truth. If we make ourselves of no reputation there is nothing to lose in the first place. Jesus was the Son of God; yet, Scripture declares that He made Himself of no reputation (Philippians 2:7). He laid His own life down that we might live. Elitism lays nothing down but its adversaries. Elitism corners men, leaving them with no way out. When they do come out swinging, elitism is there to point its bloody finger and say, "See, I told you they were evil." Simply put, elitism exalts its own ethics, deduction, and reasoning.

Ideological supremacy is far more dangerous than even racial supremacy, only in that it is able to hide itself behind pseudo-righteous causes. Currently in our country, elitism rules the media and many of our learning institutions. It is also the driving force behind evil political ideologies. Elitism first commits genocide in its heart long before it manifests itself in the natural. Elitism is the mother of all delusions, the antithesis of humility, and the spirit of the anti-Christ. Sadly, the workings of it can sometimes even be found in the Church, among those of us who believe.

Having elite tendencies does not make someone an elitist. Those may actually be God-given gifts. Elitism is the self-elevated reward elitists crown themselves with. Elitism only hears its own words, because it believes there are no words greater than its own to listen to. Humility, however, will listen for the voice of God.

Elitism creates a culture where others cannot measure up. The elitist approves whoever they approve and reject whoever they reject. They legislate their own arrogance and worship their own egos. They sacrifice the broken, the poor, the sick, the downtrodden, and the weak at the altar of their heartless god. They will sacrifice their own nation just to hear themselves speak. Then they pat each other's back and say, "Well done," while all creation groans.

The Kingdom of God, through the Spirit of Elijah, is here to fill in the valleys and bring every mountain and hill low. The evil wisdom of this age does just the opposite. It makes every valley deeper and every mountain and hill higher still. Elitism is the brazier evil puts on itself to lift, separate, and reveal its cleavage, seducing the world into a perverted stupor.

Jesus is the strong tower of the disenfranchised. Jesus is the rock of justice this world rails against. He is the victor in your battles and the healing balm of joy and strength to the brokenhearted. He is near the brokenhearted and He says, "Come" to all who are weary and heavy laden, promising rest. As we enter through these gates with thanksgiving, our deliverance and redemption draws near.

On a personal note, I, by nature, want to reach conclusions, like most of us. My personal pursuit of God is the most important thing in my life, yet, I often think myself in circles, like a dog in pursuit of his tail. Sometimes, God in His infinite wisdom and love for me, allows me to actually catch what it is I am chasing. In His love and kindness, he allows me to feel my razor-sharp teeth sink into the object I was chasing with the relentless grip of a pit bull. Then, when time seems frozen and eternal, and I find myself standing in the precarious and humiliating position with my own tail in my mouth, something wonderful happens. In that moment, I again realize I need a Savior. The "aha" moment descends upon me and I thoroughly realize the only way out this situation is to humble myself and have faith in God—like a child.

Therefore, faith truly becomes more important than my conclusions. I understand why Jesus said, "When the Son of man returns, will He really find faith on the earth?" (Luke 18:8). Proverbs suddenly becomes alive again when it says, "There is more hope for a fool than one who is wise in their own eyes (paraphrased from Proverbs 26:12). This is the circumcision of the heart that God Himself performs *for* us, not against us.

So, I am learning to enjoy the journey. Even the moments I catch what I am convinced needs catching. Surely, God uses everything for our good.

This will happen for those who are called by His name. Those who hear their Shepherd's voice and respond to it. This will happen for us in

THE CIRCUMCISION

the presence of our enemies, and the backdrop could not be better than these days for such a display of God's power and grace.

You can find more on this topic of elitism in my previous book, *The Presence Purposed Life*. I hope to write a book focused on this topic in the future. Lord willing, I will do so.

A Word to My Prophets

You truly love Me and you love My people. You love My refining fire, and endure the threshing floor. You oppose the proud and tear down their high places they love to stand in. You raise up the lowly and give them grace. You bring healing to their wounds and bind them up. You tell them about their glorious future in Me and cause them to run to their future. You help establish their identities in Me. You say what I say, and pray what I pray. They can't see you for seeing Me. My refiners fire will surely mark you, and those who receive you. That is My reward to you, and to those who receive you.

You live to hear My voice, and My voice is clear when you speak. You endure the scorn of evil and jealous men, but I say My refiners fire will rest upon you and who can stand when I come? This is the time of outpouring and glory. Set the captives free. Express My goodness so that it is clear that I am for My people. Recognize who I am in them and honor them. Qualify the disqualified. Rest in who you are, and don't apologize for who I called you to be. You are the voice and hold the rhythm of My war cadence. Hear the war drums of My Spirit. Cry out in the wilderness My mighty ones, cry out. Plunge My sword into the injustice of the enemy. Bind up the hurting and downcast. Lift the burdens off their backs imposed on them by wicked men and malevolent spirits and I will give them rest. Undo the condemnation that imprisons their hearts.

Lay the ax to the root of fallen perception in the lives of those who receive you. Unlock the gifts and callings with the keys I have given you. Bring hope to the hopeless, freedom to the captives, healing to the sick and brokenhearted, vision to the blind, and hearing to the ears of those who cannot hear! This is your hour, arise and let the Lion roar over the sheep as their protector! Tell the world of what I have done for them.

Do not fear, but be diligent to stay close to Me. Stay close to every word that proceeds from My mouth. Know My heart. Keep yourselves in humility, that will be your protection. Jezebel, Satan, and the like, would still kill you if they could. Do not fear death, but be bold and courageous. Do not try to analyze everything I ask you to say, that will only prove to be destructive. Do not be enamored by your calling because the brightness of it will blind and deafen you. Do not wander far from the threshing floor and you will see and hear as you should. I love you, so give to My sheep from that which I have given to you, and in the same gentleness. Blessed is he who is not offended because of Me. Blessed are they who are not offended because of you.

There are two houses in the garden. One I AM building—the other is built in vain. Now go and be who I AM in you, and Be who YOU ARE in ME.

A Warning to False Prophets

There are some of you who call yourselves My prophets and are not. You manipulate My sheep with craftiness and control to build your own kingdoms. You lay my little ones bare and naked, exposed to the judgments of carnal men. You say the word you speak is My word, but it is not My word, because I did not give you the words you speak. Your father gave you the words you speak, to slaughter the innocent and lay them bare. You bring confusion and you speak only to the desires of carnal men's hearts. You invoke an unholy fear, and call it the fear of the Lord. You speak in your own name, to glorify your own name. You only use My name to get into the door. Those who call themselves psychics are more honest than you, because they do not claim to speak for Me. In fact, it will be better for many of them than it will be for you in the day of judgment. I know who you are but I do not know you, because you do not know My heart. The hearts I recognize and know are the hearts that testify of Me.

Therefore, hear what the Spirit is saying and repent immediately. If you do not repent, you will be one of those who say "Lord, Lord, we prophesied in Your name, we cast out devils in Your name." And I will say back to you, "I never knew you. Depart from Me you workers of iniquity." This is your moment of grace. If I was not willing to forgive you, you would not be reading this. This is your brief moment to repent, or you will be judged according to your own works.

A SCRIPTURAL AND PROPHETIC DESCRIPTION OF REVIVAL AND REFORMATION

Earlier, I attempted to give my limited definition of *revival*. I want to take a moment to describe and define *reformation* and *restoration* as I have come to understand them.

Reformation is the act of reforming that which was once formed, while *restoration* is the act of returning something to its original unimpaired condition.

Think of an old house that was once glorious in its structure, but has become somewhat dilapidated. Let's say that the old house had one particular wing that has fallen down and no longer exists. The part that no longer exists will need *reformation*. What was once formed is no longer, and it must be reformed. The remaining, salvageable structure, on the other hand, will need *restoration*. What exists needs to be brought back to its original condition. It's all the same house, and it is all built on the same foundation. If there was a part of the structure that was not part of the original structure and not built on the original foundation, that part would be torn down and removed. And the part that is being reformed is still a part of the "restoration of all things." This describes what is happening in the global Body of Christ—to both individuals and local assemblies themselves.

Revival, reformation, and restoration all begins with the manifest presence of God. He is the builder of His temple, and while He has sent individuals who will represent Him in the process, God alone is both the Builder and the Head of that which is being built. This process is described in Scripture in the book of Malachi:

> "I will send my messenger, who will prepare the way before me. Then suddenly the Lord you are seeking will come to his temple; the messenger of the covenant, whom you desire, will come," says the Lord Almighty.
>
> But who can endure the day of his coming? Who can stand when he appears? For he will be like a refiner's fire or a launderer's soap. He will sit as a refiner and purifier of silver; he will purify the Levites and refine them like gold and silver. Then the Lord will have men who will bring offerings in righteousness, and the offerings of Judah and Jerusalem will be acceptable to the Lord, as in days gone by, as in former years.
>
> "So I will come to put you on trial. I will be quick to testify against sorcerers, adulterers and perjurers, against those who defraud laborers of their wages, who oppress the widows and the fatherless, and deprive the foreigners among you of justice, but do not fear me," says the Lord Almighty. "I the Lord do not change. So you, the descendants of Jacob, are not destroyed."
> ~ Malachi 3:1-7, NIV.

Notice how the last paragraph says that God will put us on trial. This may sound a bit unnerving, but in Christ the end result is always good. Examine how He finished this portion of Scripture: "So you, the descendants of Jacob, are not destroyed" (Malachi 3:7). The sons of Jacob are sons of promise. In the New Covenant, those born of God are the sons of promise. Though we will sense the fear of the Lord when revival is happening, we need not fear being physically consumed. However, our fallen perceptions *will* be consumed so that God's Spirit can once again be the dominant voice in our lives.

In the New Covenant, we ourselves are the temple of the Holy Spirit:

A SCRIPTURAL AND PROPHETIC DESCRIPTION OF REVIVAL AND REFORMATION

Or do you not know that your body is the temple of the Holy Spirit who is in you, whom you have from God, and you are not your own? ~ 1 Corinthians 6:19

In Malachi 3, God said He will be a quick witness and purge us of the things holding us back. Notice He also said, "For he will be like a refiner's fire or a launderer's soap. He will sit as a refiner and purifier of silver; he will purify the Levites and refine them like gold and silver" (Malachi 2:2b-3). That is good news! The purification process does not happen by men publicly shaming one another, but by an inner work of the Holy Spirit.

In the New Covenant, we stand on God's grace. It's the only leg any of us have to stand on. When the Scriptures says, "Who can stand when he appears?" (Malachi 3:2), the answer is only those who stand on the grace of God. This is the very grace that was extended to us when we believed in the finished work of Christ through the death and resurrection of Jesus. His grace, received through faith, is our only ability to stand.

Romans 5 tells us we have been made righteous through no works of our own. If we are saved apart from our own works, will not the same grace that saved us also bring God's work to completion within us? When I speak of a purging, refiner's fire, I am speaking of a purging fire at work for the purpose of transformation in us who believe. Only God can do such a thing. He does this not to hold things against us in the sense of an eternal judgment, but actually removes these things from us. We need to experience this holy move of the Lord, but we need not fear experiencing this awesome expression of God's power. Yes, more than likely some will tremble, but God will be at the helm of this ship, not man.

God's heart in this is not to destroy us, but to transform us. A clear example of what I am speaking of is found in Revelation 1. When John saw Jesus in all of His glory, he was physically terrified, but God instructed him not to fear.

"And when I saw Him, I fell at His feet as dead. But He laid His right hand on me, saying to me, "Do not be afraid; I am the First and the Last." ~ Revelation 1:17

John experienced the fear of the Lord, but Jesus reassured him by saying, "Do not be afraid; I am the First and the Last." This was another way of assuring John to keep the faith, because Jesus was the Author and the Finisher of His faith. Jesus knew that John was overwhelmed by His presence, so much so that if He hadn't reassured John, John likely would not have been able to stand before Him. Personally, I believe that when we turn our hearts to Jesus we can rest assured in knowing that Jesus is not coming to destroy us.

Malachi 3 describes the awesome presence that will be in us and upon us, both in an individual and corporate sense. When God shows up in this way, as He did to John, we will not have to conjure anything up through intimidating words. God's presence will be far more dramatic than any man can articulate or manufacture.

We will also have no need to be presumptuous. That is what Uzzah did when the Ark of the Covenant nearly fell over and he assumed he needed to step in and steady the Ark, which resulted in him dropping dead on the spot (2 Samuel 6:7). This was not just limited to the Old Testament. In the book of Acts, Ananias and Sapphira dropped dead because of their assumption and pretense (Acts 5:1-11), at the same moment Scripture declared that "great grace was among all the people" (Acts 4:33). Grace gives us every reason *not* to pretend, and teaches us a healthy fear of the Lord. Whatever we do, we want to remain honest. If God is moving in such a way, the last thing we would want to do is deny the very things His presence is revealing within us.

Refusing to operate in presumption and assumption does not mean that we will not use gifts of the Spirit to facilitate and steward what the Lord is doing in these moments. It simply means that the source will truly be the Spirit and not the flesh. We will operate out of clear direction the Lord gives us, or a strong impression we feel in our hearts as we follow Him.

A SCRIPTURAL AND PROPHETIC DESCRIPTION OF REVIVAL AND REFORMATION

Malachi 3 is clear that the Lord Himself will be a swift witness—it will not be men speaking as mere men. When mortals stand in this kind of presence, the presence of God will speak for itself. Sometimes, God will need not even speak, as people's hearts will come under arrest in a holy sense of awe.

There are times when spiritual gifts are used to confront people in impersonal, unloving, and unhealthy ways, such as calling people out in a corporate setting when it would be wiser to speak to them directly and privately. I believe that when we experience this level of God's presence, repentance will not be an issue; it will be a natural byproduct of God's sovereign work.

I believe we will see this even in our day, and the tangible, manifest presence of God will spill out of our homes and meeting places and into our cities and regions. In past revivals led by Charles Finney and others, unusual things would happen in the surrounding regions. When the Spirit of God moved in such ways, there were accounts of people entering a city (and even counties in some instances) and unsaved people in that geographical area would suddenly feel compelled to repent. Some would weep as they were overwhelmed with an immediate knowing that they needed Jesus. Only God can do these things, but He will use men whose hearts are turned to Him as a catalyst.

I believe we will also see the unspeakable joy of the Lord will be released at a whole new level. Righteousness, peace, and joy in the Holy Ghost will clearly be experienced in our hearts.

There are many moves of God, and you could even call some a "revival" or "renewal" of sorts, but what I am describing here is of another dimension. The reason I believe I have authority to say this, besides a whole lot of unction at this moment, is because as birth pangs get closer, they become more intense. Where sin abounds, grace that much more abounds. In reading about revivals of the past that affected entire regions (such as Azusa Street, Brownsville, etc.), there was a global impact that followed. I believe that this time, the Lord is going to speak for Himself to our hearts at a higher level than we have ever witnessed before.

THE PRESENT REFORMATION, CONCERNING THE CHURCH

After Pentecost, the early Church found itself in a state of spiritual vibrancy, which, over time, began to wane. This was most noticeable during the Dark Ages, though it began long before. Then came a great reformation where the Church began to build on the revelation that we're saved by grace through faith, apart from works. This reformation is credited by most to Martin Luther. Since then, we have seen the re-emergence of the importance of the Baptism of the Holy Spirit, as well as the defining attributes of different offices of ministry that are articulated in the book of Ephesians. This is sometimes called the *fivefold ministry*.

When Jesus ascended back to the Father, Ephesians 4 tells us He gave of Himself gifts to men. These gifts are called *ascension gifts* or the fivefold ministry, made up of apostles, prophets, evangelists, pastors, and teachers. Each gift is an aspect of the grace that Christ Himself walked in before He ascended to Heaven. These are not gifts of the Holy Spirit, though it is impossible to walk in the fullness of these gifts as we were intended to without the Holy Spirit. There will be nothing built by the Lord that doesn't require the involvement of His Spirit to build and sustain. It doesn't mean a person *can't* build something that doesn't require the Holy Spirit. Remember, there is only one true house the Lord is building—the other is built in vain. If Jesus followed the guidance of the Holy Spirit to fulfill His ministry on the earth, so will anyone else who is called to walk in one of these gifts.

THE PRESENT REFORMATION, CONCERNING THE CHURCH

I want to enter into this next section with my hat in my hand. I do not want to insinuate in any way that I know everything from beginning to end, far from it. I told of a visitation I had in 1997 where I heard, *Prepare the way of the Lord* three times. When I heard God speak this in my heart, I didn't even know what it meant right away. Looking back, I can see that this grace was at work in my life even before I heard the words, but I had no grid to share about this. I am still learning what it means to "prepare the way." The weekend I heard these words, I received a deep impartation that I was fully aware I could not articulate with thought or speech. It has been through the process of many years and many failures that the Lord has revealed to me what He imparted to me. At times, I'm not sure I've even scratched the surface.

I learned of the relentless love of God and His faithfulness when I believed I was unlovable and I when I was not faithful at all. When I was self-destructing, He was there. His strong hand humbled me, against my will at times I might add! I did not volunteer for the humility conference; what I have learned has come more through humiliation than cooperation, though I am learning to cooperate with God in this process and I am learning obedience through extreme suffering, just as Jesus did (Hebrews 5:8). I felt I needed to say that before I write the next portion of this book.

As believers and ministers, we testify to what we have seen and heard. We freely give what we have freely received. We do what we see God do, and we say what we hear Him say. That's the life Jesus modeled for all of us. We cannot give what we do not have. Peter told a man begging for alms, "Silver and gold have I none, but what I have I will give you" (Acts 3:6).

So often, men speak about what they *believe* they know about Jesus instead of teaching what they have seen, heard, and experienced. One is intellectual commentary on a subject, while the other is a life-giving testimony that goes deeper than intellect alone.

Jesus healed a blind man, who was then taken before a counsel. They started asking him questions about Jesus that he didn't know the answers to. I love how he replied, "All I know is, I was blind and now I see" (John 9:25). He testified to what he had seen and heard, and that was all that was required of him in that moment. What we have seen and heard is all that is required of any of us. We are witnesses to what we have seen and heard, even what we are seeing and hearing in the moment. If we haven't seen and heard, there is nothing to speak of. Whatever our ministry is, it will be built on the testimony of what we have seen and heard.

It is the witness of what we are seeing and hearing that makes the Church vibrant. When the witnesses' testimony is not there, the vibrancy of the Church will wane. Those who have been born again have already witnessed their own encounter with Jesus, or they wouldn't be born again. They have something they are witness to, and should be a witness to that they received. (If you have forgotten that moment, you might want to dust off your testimony and remember who you are.) From a certified believer to a certified apostle, all are witnesses to what they have seen and heard. One point of reformation that the Lord is restoring to His body is this truth, which has waned in some circles.

The place Jesus is taking His Church requires that we live by every word that proceeds from His mouth (Matthew 4:4). Jesus is not merely the "figurehead" of His Church; He is the literal, living "Head" of the Church. By Him, the house is built (Hebrews 3:4). He is the Author and Finisher of our faith (Hebrews 12:2) as individuals, and He is the Author and Finisher of His temple corporately. He is both the Author and the Finisher globally. The rest of us are simply willing participants, endued with the power and anointing of the Holy Spirit. Only one house is being built by the Lord—the other is built in vain.

THE PRESENT REFORMATION, CONCERNING APOSTLES

Paul never said there weren't many apostles. Instead, he said "You do not have many fathers" (1 Corinthians 4:15). There are many thoughts at large concerning apostles—who they are, what they do, what qualifies a person to be one, and so on. Allow me to speak to that. The first thing I can say about an apostle is, "He ain't from around here!" Yes, he could be your next-door neighbor, but he doesn't actually live next door; he lives in the secret place before the Lord. He lives to do what he sees his Lord do and to say what he hears his Lord say. His purpose is to reflect Christ, not his apostleship. Apostles have become a dime a dozen, but to reflect Christ is priceless, and is the ultimate prize for a true apostle. He fully understands that an encounter with Jesus is the only thing that has ever changed anyone. He doesn't come to plant a church, because he knows the Church has already been planted, and there is only one true Church. Rather, he comes to *establish* that which was planted on the day of Christ's death, burial, and resurrection. He knows that the church he is sent to establish in doctrine is not built by the hands of men, but by the very breath of God.

He doesn't seek to learn what an apostle is in an attempt to act accordingly. He was called to be an apostle before he was in his mother's womb. He seeks first the Kingdom from which he was born first, above all things, and in doing so he cannot help but reflect the apostolic mantle, because it is just who he is. It was never a decision he could make alone; the decision was made by God before he was ever born.

He holds within his heart blueprints that he knows are not his. Thoughts that he knows are not from his own reasoning. He is gripped by the strong hand of God for a divine purpose. He is a well that will bring increase to those around him. All who draw from this well will be spiritually bigger, stronger, and faster. They will experience increase.

He doesn't come in his own name or on his own accord, because he is sent to be a messenger of the covenant by following "the Messenger" of the covenant, and impart the foundation of that covenant in the hearts of men. Signs and wonders will follow everywhere his feet tread. He is a gift that Christ Himself gave.

He is intended to be a cultural icon of Heaven that reveals and establishes the culture of Heaven here to us on earth. He, as well as the prophet, are catalysts for corporate transformation and change.

There are some myths floating around about the roles and position of apostles that are not totally accurate. Some believe that a person is not apostolic unless they have planted a church, but I would like to challenge that. Jesus never started a local assembly when He walked the earth, and most who followed Him left before it was all said and done. Instead, Jesus planted Himself when He laid His life down for us; He planted "the Church," being the Church contained in seed form. Through His death and burial, the seed was planted. His resurrection brought forth this seed from the ground, and everything that has been built has been hidden in Him and upon Him as the Cornerstone of the Church. We are hidden in Christ; therefore, the Church is hidden in Christ.

Many apostles in authority today are leaders in local churches they didn't plant. Someone else planted the work, and they were either recognized by the local assembly to impart apostolic revelation, or they overthrew the leadership of the local assembly and took over in the name of their own authority. Not good. As I have heard it said, when you have to manipulate to gain access, you will have to continue to manipulate in order to keep access. This is true with any dishonest effort we make for our own gain. Unless the Lord builds the house, the house is built in vain.

THE PRESENT REFORMATION, CONCERNING APOSTLES

Those who will walk fully in apostolic authority or any other authority, will be those who contend for God's presence rather than their own. They are first when it comes to demonstrating the government of God. Everything they do will point to Christ and Him crucified. They will model and demonstrate the life God intended for all of us to walk in. They will establish us in the doctrines of Christ, but not the baloney some are trying to establish us in. They are equipped to impart to us the grace they have been given, and to equip us to walk in the same.

Many of those in apostolic ministry proclaim themselves to be "fathers in the faith." If this is true, they should demonstrate this by turning their hearts to the children, rather than insisting the children turn their hearts to them. In Malachi, the order of these things is that Elijah will turn the hearts of the fathers *first*, then the children. Therefore, this reformation will accelerate when those who are fathers turn their hearts to their children—both biological and spiritual. The role of a spiritual father is not exclusive to those who are apostolic. In fact, anyone can function in this role. All Christians should mature to that of a father or mother in the Spirit.

However, the one in an apostolic office should reflect a father's heart and role to his children. As fathers, we create an environment for our children to succeed in. We raise our children, cheer them on, educate them, and, one day, send them out. When we send them, they are sent out as our children. This means that when they need us, we are there for them. When they get in a mess, we help them. When they lose their way, we bring them back to the foundation they are built upon. We are the shoulders for them to stand on. If they choose to go to college, and we are able to fund it, we should do so. If we can't, we help as we are able. We are mindful of our children, whether they are in our house or elsewhere. We are the one place they should know they can come to for help when they need it. They should be able to depend on these things. When they need to learn to deal with something without our involvement, we should recognize that as well. This is all simply what fathers do.

If you are indeed a father in the Spirit, you should be laying up for your children, not demanding your children to lay up for you. Don't ask your sons and daughters to "pay up" to you, then accuse them of having an orphan spirit when they can't. Paul didn't say there were too many orphans, he said there weren't many fathers.

> Now for the third time I am ready to come to you. And I will not be burdensome to you; for I do not seek yours, but you. For the children ought not to lay up for the parents, but the parents for the children. ~ 2 Corinthians 12:14

If Simon, who was a Sorcerer, was aggressively rebuked by Peter for thinking the Holy Spirit was something he could purchase, how much more will the Lord's anger be toward someone who claims to be both a father and an apostle who does the same thing? Don't think the Lord is impressed with charging sons and daughters for what you have been freely given. Yet, many lead sons and daughters to believe their covering and blessing is something that should be sought, bought, and paid for consistently. In some circles, if a son can't pay up, he is rebuked. What kind of father charges his sons and daughters a fee for being their father in the first place? This is Jesus speaking to Peter in Matthew.

> When they had come to Capernaum, those who received the temple tax came to Peter and said, "Does your Teacher not pay the temple tax?"
> He said, "Yes."
> And when he had come into the house, Jesus anticipated him, saying, "What do you think, Simon? From whom do the kings of the earth take customs or taxes, from their sons or from strangers?"
> Peter said to Him, "From strangers."
> Jesus said to him, "Then the sons are free."
> ~Matthew 17:24-26

THE PRESENT REFORMATION, CONCERNING APOSTLES

This has nothing to do with conferences, church tithes, fundraisers, or ministry schools. This is referring specifically to the relationship between those who call themselves spiritual fathers with their sons and daughters. This relationship is different than other relationships. When you take the responsibility to call yourself the father of another, this relationship is of another level, for another purpose. If a son or daughter wants to bless you, that is awesome, but to require it? That's something altogether different.

If you claim to be an apostolic father in the Spirit, and the systems you build provide you with a security that you cannot walk away from, then your heart has been hijacked by your systems, and is not turned to your sons and daughters. To take it a step further, if you can't walk away from the kind of system I described, you may actually be worshipping your system as well. If this is so, then you need to turn your heart to God and repent. If He wasn't ready to forgive you, you wouldn't be reading this sentence. This is your moment to be who He has called you to be, and to give what He has called you to give. As I said earlier, if you are going to be a builder in *the* House the Lord is building, you must first *be* a house the Lord is building.

Some call their networks and associations "a family," yet they are built through common business models that resemble pyramid systems at best and Ponzi schemes at worst. Therein, the esteemed relationship between fathers and sons is based on a business arrangement; if the son pays, the father proclaims that his heart is turned to him and calls it "love." The problem is not that some of these men are false apostles, though Paul warns of false apostles. Rather, the problem is that these men do not fully demonstrate the true heart of the Father. For some, the systems they have created have allowed them to think far more highly of themselves than they ought, and the systems themselves have become a burden on the backs of their children that they themselves will not bear.

Because of God's goodness, He has still moved in some of these circles to some extent, but it is time for some to hear what the Spirit is saying—and quickly. Turn your hearts to your children, because if they truly are your children, you are held responsible by your own proclamation of being their father.

There are ministries currently here in the United States that are modeling a newer wineskin, with obvious results. They often come in slightly under the radar, yet a clearer picture is developing because of their existence. When the hearts of fathers are turned to the children and not their own systems, reformation will speed up and come upon the body at a faster pace. Some of those in apostolic circles will be offended by this notion. However, some will see this and run in the wisdom of it. I do not desire to be an offense to anyone, nor is having to be anything to be proud of, but I cannot ignore these things and still sleep at night. I wouldn't call myself a perfect father by any stretch of the imagination, but I do have a heart that desires to be. As Arthur Burt once said, "We have to be willing to be made willing." We have to start there.

> And He Himself gave some to be apostles, some prophets, some evangelists, and some pastors and teachers, for the equipping of the saints for the work of ministry, for the edifying of the body of Christ, till we all come to the unity of the faith and of the knowledge of the Son of God, to a perfect man, to the measure of the stature of the fullness of Christ. ~ Ephesians 4:11-13

> Now, therefore, you are no longer strangers and foreigners, but fellow citizens with the saints and members of the household of God, having been built on the foundation of the apostles and prophets, Jesus Christ Himself being the chief cornerstone, in whom the whole building, being fitted together, grows into a holy temple in the Lord, in whom you also are being built together for a dwelling place of God in the Spirit. ~ Ephesians 2:19-22

Apostles, prophets, evangelists, pastors and teachers hold specific roles for equipping the saints. Every believer has gifts and callings within them. While not all called to an equipping office of ministry, all are called to the ministry of reconciliation (2 Corinthians 5:18), and that in itself should be seen as a reason to stay ready in season and out of season. *All* are called to give what they were freely given, and to testify to what they have seen and heard. That means we should be ready at all times to do what we see Jesus do and say what we hear Him say. All gifts do not just pertain to inside the walls of the church, although all of the Church and the world will be blessed by the results of those who walk in that which they were called to do. When healthy leadership is present, these gifts and callings will emerge and flourish.

I could say more about the reforming work I see the Lord doing in apostolic circles, but I believe if what I have said will be received into the hearts of those who hear, many of the issues we face will take care of themselves.

While it is important to receive a prophet in the name of a prophet to obtain the prophet's reward, it is just as important to receive an apostle in the name of an apostle for the same reason. That doesn't necessarily mean one should wear their title like a badge. There are some who publicly hold the title, that doesn't in itself make them a true or false apostle. All the world sees are *Christians*. They don't care about titles and commissions, nor should they have to. Some of the most effective apostolic ministry being displayed is through folks who rarely, if ever, speak about it publicly. Jesus didn't mind people wondering and guessing who He was, and we shouldn't, either. If it is not revealed to others by the Spirit of God, one revealing their title without receiving a Spirit-led unction to do so probably will not help. Peter knew Jesus was the Messiah by the Spirit of God and still denied Him three times.

Many of us supply our best to humanity when we don't pretend to know all the answers. When we can't really say we know exactly where we are going, or exactly what it will look like, we just know we are going by each step revealed. Again, we have no choice but to humble ourselves under the mighty hand of God. We arrive to a clear end through a mysteriously wonderful journey of steps. Each one taken in faith. Each one requiring risk. Each step that is ordered by the Lord. So individually and corporately we have to be satisfied with our parts, and our steps. We need to love each one, because it is our journey, and we need to love and be thankful we have a journey. What would life be without one?

A Word to My Apostles

Truly you love Me, and you love My people. You put them before yourself. You choose to lay down your life for them and you desire that they exceed you, and do greater works than you do. You are my apostles who love the least, who love My little ones. You wipe away the tears of abuse and heal the brokenhearted. When My people are around you, they feel free to fly away with Me. They want to run to Me. They want to worship Me, because when they see you, they see Me. They want to love Me because of you! You truly are My apostles, because they cannot see you for seeing Me. You live and move and have your being in Me, so much so, that they can no longer see where you end and I begin! You point to the door for them to enter in where you already are. You dine with Me and you always bring your guests, My little ones. You do not leave them behind, and are always thoughtful of them. You choose to be last if it will first lead them to Me.

You are My apostles who I first gave of Myself. You are my champions for this next season, because it is no longer you that lives, but I Myself live in you, through you, and upon you. You see Me as the prize, and you are My prize as it is with all My children. Now bring those to yourself who are weak and heavy laden, and I will give them rest through you. You serve Me in your weakness. You cover the naked. You testify of Me and death does not scare you. You are a breath of fresh air. Now set My people free, and deliver them from the bondage of unreasonable men and malevolent spirits. Undo the works of the devil. Heal the sick, raise the dead, give sight to the blind, and open the deaf ears. You are sons of My thunder and lightnings, so do not withhold My sword, but swing it with all I give you. You are blessed.

The first shall be last and the last shall be first. If I called you first it is because you are to be the first to demonstrate what it means to be last. You

THE PRESENT REFORMATION, CONCERNING APOSTLES

were called first to demonstrate what it means to be one who loves Me with all of your heart, all of your soul, all of your strength, all of your mind, and then your neighbor as yourself. You should be the first to do what you see Me do and first to say what you hear Me say. You should be first to love, first to forgive, first to reconcile, first to heal, first to deliver, and first to bring freedom. Yet, some of you have turned My children into beggars, denying them grace, always positioning yourself for others to beg you for your mercy, forgiveness, and restoration.

Did I not say the greatest among you will be the greatest servant, yet some of you have chosen to make yourselves first when I have already graced you first. You sit among yourselves to decide who the greatest in the Kingdom is, fretting over your position of being first when I called you to be the first to choose being last. Should calamity fall against a house would a good father not want the calamity to fall upon himself to spare his wife and children? Yet some of you will sacrifice your own children to assure you remain first. You will be first alright.

In the restoration of all things, have I not chosen to restore you last, to demonstrate the first shall be last? If you make yourselves first, will you not be the first ones I chasten? If I learned obedience as the Son through My sufferings, how will you escape? Were you not called to be a son first?

You are called to be first to love, first to bring joy, first to bring peace, first to show forbearance, first to be kind, first to reveal My goodness, first to be faithful, first to be gentle, and first to demonstrate self-control. Then to demonstrate who I AM with My heart, with signs and wonders, building on the foundation I laid. Yet, some of you have laid your own foundation and gone out in your own name as a master builder, but where were you when I laid the foundations of the earth? Who sent you this way?

Some of you have become the first to disqualify those I have qualified, and you have lifted yourselves above all others, drawing all men to you. You make yourselves the last word, when I AM the Finisher. Did you not see in the end of My ministry how I was lifted up? I was beaten, stripped naked before men, crowned with thorns, and yet, was I not first? Who are you? Who sent you this way?

I came to undo the works of the devil, now I will send Elijah to undo your works, and restore all things.

If you cry out for repentance in others, will you not be first to demonstrate? Know what it means to be first. Know what it means to love. Know what it means to humble yourself. Know what it means to be last before others, and you will demonstrate what it means to be first.

There are currently two houses in the garden. One I AM building—the other is built in vain. One is wheat and one is tares and they grow together. There is nothing common between them. When the final harvest comes My reapers will first gather together the tares and bind them in bundles to burn them, and they will gather the wheat into my barn.

Now go and be who I AM in you, and Be who YOU ARE in ME.

For I think that God has displayed us, the apostles, last, as men condemned to death; for we have been made a spectacle to the world, both to angels and to men. We are fools for Christ's sake, but you are wise in Christ! We are weak, but you are strong! You are distinguished, but we are dishonored! To the present hour we both hunger and thirst, and we are poorly clothed, and beaten, and homeless. And we labor, working with our own hands. Being reviled, we bless; being persecuted, we endure; being defamed, we entreat. We have been made as the filth of the world, the offscouring of all things until now.

I do not write these things to shame you, but as my beloved children I warn you. For though you might have ten thousand instructors in Christ, yet you do not have many fathers; for in Christ Jesus I have begotten you through the gospel. Therefore I urge you, imitate me. ~ 1 Corinthians 4:9-16

To learn more about false apostles, I would recommend reading 2 Corinthians 11. It is a relatively short chapter, but Paul gives characteristics that will help one recognize false apostles.

THE PRESENT REFORMATION, CONCERNING APOSTLES

The Apostle

The apostle didn't start with eyes to see.
He was persecuting all the sons,
Struck blind by the mighty one.
The way he was, he knew was done.
As lost as one could be.
The apostle knew that everything had changed.
He was learning 'bout humility,
His eyes were blind but he could see.
He found himself upon his knees.
His world was rearranged.
The Lord would send a man to bring relief.
So he waited on the straightened street.
The man would pray and Saul would see.
This chosen man who caused such grief,
A former enemy.
The apostle saw what he'd be suffering.
He knew he had to count the cost,
To save his head or save the lost.
Deny himself and grab his cross,
There was no in between.
The apostle Paul forsook his liberty.
He had to bear his rule in chains.
A slave he said, yet how he reigned,
Not much with speech, but power enflamed,
He was a king and priest.
The apostle didn't build no pyramids.
He learned that those were just the tombs
A Pharaoh's buried in.
The apostle did not sell his covering.
No what he had could not be bought.
The Spirit present must be caught.
His sons were those who could be taught,

THE HOUSE THAT JESUS BUILT

To be an offering.
The apostle didn't charge his sons a dime.
What kind of father would he be,
Protecting children for a fee?
He freely gave what he received.
A gift unlocked when they believed.
A father for all times.
The apostle didn't build things with his hands.
A master builder, God ordained,
The Spirit builds or it's in vain,
He lays it down in Jesus name,
With blueprints and with plans.
Jesus crucified is what he preached.
He demonstrated what it was,
To forge ahead without a pause.
No looking back his only cause,
The outcast he could reach.
The apostle did not boast in his own strength.
No, he chose to tell us 'bout a thorn,
The strength of God in weakness born,
How he was beaten, scourged, and scorned,
His love it had no lengths.
The apostle took a trip when he was warned.
Snake-bit, shackled, frowned upon,
Stoned and left for dead, forlorn,
Despising life at times he mourned.
In weakness, he found strength.
The apostle said he reckoned himself dead.
The life he lived was not his own.
He found his power at the throne,
The throne of grace to him belonged,
The life of Christ revealed.
The apostle sometimes spoke of his reward.
For all the troubles and the chains,

THE PRESENT REFORMATION, CONCERNING APOSTLES

To live is Christ, to die is gain,
Those were the words that he proclaimed.
His Master he adored.
The apostle stood before a listening king.
He spoke so boldly without shame.
Not for money, or for fame,
No dropping other people's names,
Except that of his Lord.
The apostle finally lost his head it seems.
Least that's the story I've been told.
He ran the race so fierce and bold.
A fighter Satan couldn't hold.
He was a king and priest.
Now apostles have a model they can see.
He wasn't kidding when he said,
"Imitate me."

WHY WAS JESUS SENT?

When we read the Bible, we read about apostles, prophets, evangelists, pastors and teachers, and about God's messenger Elijah coming back before the dreadful day of the Lord. In all of this, the big picture could get overwhelming. So, before we try to tackle all of these questions that may arise, we must go back to the beginning of the Church, after Jesus was crucified. As the Scripture says, "Jesus was the firstborn of many brethren" (Romans 8:29).

Let's start by answering the question, "Why was Jesus sent?"

> "For God so loved the world that He gave His only begotten Son, that whoever believes in Him should not perish but have everlasting life. For God did not send His Son into the world to condemn the world, but that the world through Him might be saved.
>
> "He who believes in Him is not condemned; but he who does not believe is condemned already, because he has not believed in the name of the only begotten Son of God." ~ John 3:16-18

From this Scripture, it is clear that God sent His Son because He loved us, wanted to save us from perishing, and desired to give us eternal life. This is the reason Jesus was sent, but how would He do this? The answer is found in these Scriptures:

> Now all things are of God, who has reconciled us to Himself through Jesus Christ, and has given us the ministry of

WHY WAS JESUS SENT?

reconciliation, that is, that God was in Christ reconciling the world to Himself, not imputing their trespasses to them, and has committed to us the word of reconciliation. Now then, we are ambassadors for Christ, as though God were pleading through us: we implore you on Christ's behalf, be reconciled to God. For He made Him who knew no sin to be sin for us, that we might become the righteousness of God in Him. ~ 2 Corinthians 5:18-21

For by grace you have been saved through faith, and that not of yourselves; it is the gift of God, not of works, lest anyone should boast. ~ Ephesians 2:8-9

We now have the basic answers to why God sent His Son to do an eternal work on behalf of those who believe in Him. The next question to explore is how Jesus saw His job description, if you will. The answer is contained in Jesus' own words:

"The Spirit of the Lord is upon Me, because He has anointed Me to preach the gospel to the poor; He has sent Me to heal the brokenhearted, to proclaim liberty to the captives and recovery of sight to the blind, to set at liberty those who are oppressed; to proclaim the acceptable year of the Lord." ~ Luke 4:18-19

This Scripture tells us Jesus' heart was turned to the poor, the prisoners, the blind, and the oppressed, both literally and metaphorically in circumstance. His heart was to recover that which was lost in people. His mission was to bring, good news, freedom, sight, and to proclaim the year of the Lord's favor. He mentioned "freedom" two different times.

"The thief does not come except to steal, and to kill, and to destroy. I have come that they may have life, and that they may have it more abundantly." ~ John 10:10

> Stand fast therefore in the liberty by which Christ has made us free, and do not be entangled again with a yoke of bondage.
> ~ Galatians 5:1

Christ came to give us abundant life; He came to set us free in every area of our lives—freedom to see, to prosper, to love, freedom from condemnation, freedom from those who would put us in bondage. Freedom for the sake of freedom! That is good news. That is who you are called to be, and he who the Son sets free is free indeed (John 8:36).

The foundation we have been built upon is a foundation of good news, eternal life, sight, freedom, healing, recovery, restoration, and abundance, just to name a few.

Jesus' ministry on the earth was perfect theology. He demonstrated perfect theology. He was called the stone the builders rejected, which became the Cornerstone (Acts 4:11).

WHAT IS A CORNERSTONE?

Here's a bit of history. In the days of Christ, every building that was built was completely dependent on beginning with a perfectly shaped cornerstone—perfectly squared with absolute perfect corners, surfaces, and edges. The perfection of everything built around it relied solely on the perfection of the cornerstone itself as well as the perfection in which it was laid into the ground. It had to be set perfectly level and square. If the cornerstone was not perfect, the rest of the foundation would not be, either. The "squareness" of the walls depended on the cornerstone. Every angle and pitch relied on the perfection of the cornerstone and how it was laid.

This is why Scripture uses the analogy of a cornerstone to describe Jesus, knowing the people who heard these words would understand the eternal foundation that was laid through His life. Jesus is the cornerstone that the builders rejected. He took our lives of sin and death upon Himself, becoming our sin. We, along with our sin, died with Him, were buried with Him, and we were raised with Him and seated with Him in Heavenly places. We are hidden in Him. We no longer live, and the life we now live is His. We reap where we haven't sown. Jesus took upon Himself what *we* deserved so that we could reap the harvest *He* deserved. We reap according to the seed He has sown. He delivered us, healed us, redeemed us, and finished us. Everything that pertains to life and godliness, He has placed inside of us. For freedoms' sake, He came to set us free. There are many other expressions of what He did, but these are enough to show us what Jesus' works look like.

The point of Christianity has always been the miracle of dying with

Christ and being raised with Him, and, ultimately, being seated with Him in heavenly places. Not by our works, but by His finished work of the cross. Not because we were ever good, but because He is good. Not by holding our sins against us, but by forgiving our sins once and for all. Not so we could boast in our theology and excellence, but that we, as Paul, could boast in our weaknesses and Christ's finished work.

God is Love. God reconciled the world to Himself through Christ. Christ was called the "Chief Cornerstone" and we are described as "living stones," joined together with Christ and built upon into a spiritual house (1 Peter 2:5). Since God is love, Love governs everything that is built. To be built upon Love we must be in Love, just as we are in Christ.

Reformation should always reflect the Cornerstone. If we're not careful, our revelation could simply become another law—an 'apostolic' law of expectation that we put men under, a law that produces death. We will make them "twice the devil" we are if that's what is in our hearts (Matthew 23:15), and we will load their backs with burdens we ourselves are unwilling to bear (Matthew 23:4). That is why we must be careful how we build upon that which has already been established long before any of us ever showed up.

Matthew 4 gives the account of Jesus being tempted by Satan, who ultimately took Jesus high up on a mountain where he showed Him all of the kingdoms of the world. He then told Him, "All of this can be yours if you will bow down and worship me" (Matthew 4:9). This was extreme pride and arrogance on the part of the enemy to believe he was capable of such things, but he was deceived by his own pride; therefore, everything he offered was in fact a lie. He had no intentions of grandeur for anyone but himself.

Eerily enough, I have heard these same kinds of presentations made before in the backrooms of churches. Some have made the same kinds of promises in the same spirit of pride. I believe much of this is in ignorance—or at least I hope this is the case—but I can't help but notice many who say these things call themselves "apostles."

WHAT IS A CORNERSTONE?

A Vision and Word Concerning the Cornerstone

I had a vision that was simple in sight. However, when the Lord later spoke to what I saw, the vision became alive, and what it began to reveal was extraordinary. I saw a living cell, much like what you would see in a science book concerning biology. As I was looking at the cell, it reproduced before my eyes, creating a second cell. One cell came from the other, and the two cells were stuck together. They began to reproduce, becoming a clump of cells, and I could begin to see life being formed into existence. I believe the Lord gave me a glimpse of the body being formed or built.

Remember when Gabriel spoke of the coming Christ child to Mary? A woman conceives when a seed enters the egg in her womb. The egg quickly becomes living cells joined together. As this happens, the embryo is quickly formed into cells that are joined together to become the baby that will be carried through all three trimesters. In the case with Mary, the seed was the Word of God, and the Word entered the egg in Mary's womb when she was mysteriously overshadowed. The egg quickly formed cells from the DNA of its source, and life multiplied and became flesh. The Word became flesh. That is a limited, but basic picture of how the body of Christ was hidden in Mary and formed in her womb until the appointed time of birth.

The Lord then spoke to me saying, *A mystery is being revealed. All of my children born of Me are hidden in Me. They are hidden in Me, and I am hidden in them. In the beginning I AM, and I became flesh. Before I was made flesh, I was hidden in Mary, and Mary birthed Me into the earth, and I dwelt a while among you. I AM became flesh in your presence, and you beheld Me. Then I AM crucified, then I AM buried in the tomb, then I AM resurrected. When I was crucified, you were crucified. When I was buried, you were buried. When I was resurrected, you were resurrected with Me. When I was seated at My Father's right hand, you were seated with Me in Heavenly places, because you are hidden in Me. All that I AM is in you, and all that you are is in Me. This is the mystery revealed from Me through you.*

When I AM revealed to you. You are revealed and transformed by I AM you see. Then you emerge from Me, and I emerge from you, because you are hidden in Me and I AM hidden in you. I birthed you from Me, and you birth that which is of Me from you into the earth. For the very words that proceed from Me are in you, and you release that which comes from Me into the earth. I reveal Myself and am continually revealing Myself to you. When I AM revealed to you, you are revealed and are being revealed. When this happens, it is on earth as it is in Heaven. All things are held together by My word because I AM He who was with God in the beginning of all things. Everything created was created by Me, through me, and for Me. All that I have is yours, and because you were bought with a price, all that you have is Mine. This is the mystery revealed from ME through you.

Because I have fellowship with you, you have fellowship with Me. Because I first Loved you, you love Me. I AM the Author and Finisher of your faith. I AM who I say I AM, because I AM who I AM, and I cannot lie. I AM in you and You ARE in Me. Just as I prayed it would be in John's gospel. I AM the Cornerstone, and every stone that is living is hidden in Me. As you have been birthed through Me, you are joined with Me, because You ARE in Me, and I AM in you. This is the mystery revealed from Me through you.

Who You ARE is who all creation groans to see manifested. Who You Are is birthing who I AM into the earth. You ARE the womb of Heaven, because You ARE in Me. Where My Spirit is, there is unity. Where My Spirit is, there is life. Where My Spirit is, there is freedom. Where two or more are gathered in My name, there I AM in the midst of who They ARE, because They ARE in Me. Apart from Me they can do nothing. This is the mystery revealed from Me through you.

The mystery from Me is revealed through every joint that gives life from Me to all of My body. Living stones birthed from Me as their Cornerstone joined together with Me as the living stones of My Temple. As life giving cells they reproduce the life They ARE in Me.

Did Ezekiel not see this when he prophesied over your dry bones? Did he not see an army? Did he not prophesy, "I will make breath enter you, and you will come to life?" That I will attach tendons to you and make flesh come

WHAT IS A CORNERSTONE?

upon you and cover you with skin? That I will put breath in you, and you will come to life, so that you will know that I am the Lord. Did he not hear a noise, and a rattling sound? Did he not see your bones come together and your tendons and flesh appear on you and skin cover you? Yet when there was still no breath in you, did he not prophesy to the breath, 'Come breath from the four winds?' And did they not breathe life into you that you may live? Did He not see you and all of those like you rise as a vast army coming to life and stand to your feet? Surely, He did, and truly this is so, and so it is and will be with all who are born of Me.

There are currently two houses in the garden. One I AM building—the other is built in vain. Now go and be who I AM in you, and Be who YOU ARE in Me.

This is the heart of God to us who believe, from the very cornerstone that the builders rejected. He is the House not made by hands. We are hidden in Him and everything we are is from Him. We are sent into this world as ambassadors of His Kingdom. He is Jesus Christ the hope of Glory, the Son of Man, the Son of God, in whom all the whole family of Heaven and earth are named. He is the glorified One. Forever and ever, Amen.

THE ARMY OF THE LORD

Believe it or not, there is a war, and you were born right in the middle of it. Not between what we have previously perceived as good and evil, but rather between that which truly is life and that which truly is death. The good news for us is; the battle belongs to the Lord, in fact, because of the finished work of Christ, the war has been won. Jesus said, *"It is finished."* He wasn't kidding. Because we are seated with Him, we live from the place of victory. The evil we see and experience now is a reality that is passing away before our eyes. It is a reality of all things that once held power over us, in the vain attempt to tell another story. It has a pre-determined disposition because of Jesus. Jesus is the way, the truth, and the life. Therefore, anything that paints a different picture than the one Jesus said is finished is only a fading reality that's passing away along with time.

Even so, when the enemy can seduce us, and bring us into fear, doubt, hopelessness, and unbelief, he can still inflict damage to us causing casualties. We essentially give him authority that to do so by our forgetting who we are in Christ, what He has done, and who He is in us.

Though it is finished for us by faith, we are being finished, and for those born of the Spirit, we can and may experience temporary casualties. I say temporary, because even in death, death cannot hold the children of God. We do experience the brunt of warfare at times, and it produces loss not only to ourselves, but to those who know and love us. It is the ravages of sin at work in the earth. That is why we need Jesus, and we need to stay close to Him.

God is raising up an army—His army. The army of the Lord, built by the living prophetic Word of His voice and the life-giving breath of His Spirit. When you think of spiritual battles and conflicts, remember that the wheat and the tares grow together in the same field (Matthew 13:24-30). There are two houses in our garden. One is built by the Lord—the other is built in vain.

Several years ago, I was having a conversation with my neighbor as we sat on his front porch one evening. Before I stepped into full-time ministry, I spent most of my years working in law enforcement. My neighbor was a former member of Seal Team Six, who was actually wounded in the battle of Mogadishu, depicted in the movie *Black Hawk Down*. We were sharing war stories when he looked at me and said something profound, which has stuck with me all these years.

He said, and I paraphrase, "You know, Ken, it's easy to lead someone into their first battle, because they have never experienced the harsh reality of bullets flying at them, seeing their buddy get wounded or killed, or perhaps being wounded themselves. It's the second, third, and fourth battle when you see what a soldier is made of."

From my years in law enforcement, I understood a measure of what he was talking about. I had left this field for ministry about six years prior, and, interestingly enough, it was in the ministry arena that I experienced my first *real* conflict. I was so pummeled by that experience that I wanted to quit. I even made the statement that I never wanted to call myself a "minister" ever again.

In law enforcement, my enemies were obvious, and I was trained, equipped, and capable of handling them. I had responded to many harsh and dangerous calls, and seen some horrible things. I had been through many conflicts that affected me deeply. However, when I stepped into ministry, I suddenly found myself in a new and unfamiliar place, full of naivety and delusional expectations. I was strong and had God on my side. Yet, when the spiritual bullets started flying, I was suddenly aware that I was following an invisible God and fighting against an invisible enemy. There were giants in the land! Enemies that manifested themselves at times through people I thought were fighting *with* me. It was my first experience in battle, and I didn't know who was an enemy and who was an ally.

I found that some of the people telling me who I needed to watch out for were actually themselves the ones who I really needed to watch out for! After a few bouts in this new theater of battle, I didn't want any more to do with it. I didn't trust anyone to lead me anywhere. It took me a few years to overcome the first encounter, but here's the deal: The real battle was not as much the convoluted experience that seemed so bad. Wounded though I was, the real battle was getting back up again. The real battle was softening my heart again toward those who let me down. The real issue was learning to trust again, to love and forgive again. The real battle of my first conflict was overcoming the feeling of being left spiritually paralyzed.

Make no mistake, it requires the strong hand of a loving God in our lives to do the impossible, and to change our hearts after we feel that we've been thrown under the bus by those we shared a foxhole with. But it is in these experiences that soldiers begin to be formed, where we see what we are made of.

It was when Paul was chained to a Roman Soldier under house arrest, awaiting his execution, that he wrote much of the Scripture we esteem today. It was when Stephen was being stoned that he looked up and saw a door open in the heavens and the Lord stand to His feet. It was when Jesus was being crucified that He said, "Father forgive them, they don't know what they are doing" (Luke 23:34). Some of us have a hard time loving others on our best days, but these men loved on their worst days, while under fire. This is the character you find in a true soldier of the Lord. Without God, it is impossible. However, with God, all things are possible.

God is raising up his sons and daughters in this hour, many of whom are battle-weary from one fight after another. Though they fear and tremble, they have survived and are ready to face the next fight. They don't do this from a place of pride in their own strength, but from the low place of total dependence on God. They have been thoroughly convinced of their weaknesses, yet they have been firmly established in the love and power of the Lord.

I believe this word is for some who are young and just stepping out into ministry. I believe it is also for some of you who did step out, but as many before you, found yourself stuck between the first conflict and the possibility of future battles. I believe this is a confirming word for some of you who have girded yourselves up for many battles over the course of your life and know what it means, on some level, to be a soldier.

THERE IS ONLY ONE BODY

There is only one Body in Christ, the fruit of which is of and by one Spirit—individuals who live from every word that proceeds from the mouth of God. Yet, within the Body there are many who are divided from each other because of the streams of revelation they are camped out by and found their identity in. Much of the body tends to live to debate rather than for the One they debate about. I'm not speaking of "wheat" and "tares," I am speaking of those who were called by His name yet divide themselves from their fellow brothers and sisters in the faith.

The Body of Christ should not reduce any part of itself to that of an "ism," whether it be Calvinism, Arminianism, Catholicism, Lutheranism, Methodistism, Baptistism, Presbyterianism, Fundamentalism, Anglicanism, Quakerism, Universalism, Mormanism, Pentecostalism, Protestantism, Evangelicalism, McArthurism, Osteenism, Johnsonism, Duplantisism, Copelandism, or any other *ism*. As God "IS," so is the Body. Everything else is but an "ism." This in no way implies that any of these are not part of the Body, though some of them are not. Read what the apostle Paul says about this:

> And I, brethren, could not speak to you as to spiritual people but as to carnal, as to babes in Christ. I fed you with milk and not with solid food; for until now you were not able to receive it, and even now you are still not able; for you are still carnal. For where there are envy, strife, and divisions among you, are you not carnal and behaving like mere men? For when one says, "I am of Paul," and another, "I am of Apollos," are you not carnal?

THERE IS ONLY ONE BODY

Who then is Paul, and who is Apollos, but ministers through whom you believed, as the Lord gave to each one? I planted, Apollos watered, but God gave the increase. So then neither he who plants is anything, nor he who waters, but God who gives the increase. Now he who plants and he who waters are one, and each one will receive his own reward according to his own labor. For we are God's fellow workers; you are God's field, you are God's building. ~ 1 Corinthians 3:1-9

When we view the Body in a carnal manner, we are not viewing it correctly. In the Body of Christ, when one reigns, all reign. When one hurts, all hurt.

No matter what revelation has been imparted to me, or how I have believed I had it all figured out, I have found God to be bigger still. Bigger than my current wisdom. Bigger than my current discernment. Bigger than my abilities. Bigger than the power I possess. Bigger than the wealth I hold or do not hold. Always a mystery still. The more I learn, the more mysterious He is, yet leaving a solid foundation to stand upon. Never leaving me hopeless. Never leaving me faithless. Never leaving me an orphan. Never leaving me. Constantly confounding my reasoning. Constantly revealing His grace. Constantly expanding my borders. Constantly increasing my thoughts. Relentlessly shaping me. Relentlessly cutting away the useless. Relentlessly loving me. Relentlessly forging me into His likeness.

Wrestling with conflict, I try to lay hold of Him, but when I think I have, one swift move and I'm pinned to the floor. Yet, I hold on tightly, contending for His blessing (as Jacob did in Genesis 32). I may get up with a limp, but I *will* be blessed. He's made me wise and He's let me think at times I might be a fool. He's made me strong in weakness and wise in foolishness. He has given me sight in my blindness, reason in my confusion, and with all He has done and given, He is bigger still.

I have never seen a broken and contrite heart arguing over theology. As I have heard Bill Johnson say, "Jesus Christ is perfect theology."

Jesus never gave His opinion concerning the Father, because there is no authority in an opinion. Jesus didn't come to have a debate; He came to end the debate. Jesus is not returning to validate us; He has already done that through the cross. Jesus does not compete for what He has already won; He reigns as the Champion. He's not for sale, so He can't be bought. He is the King of kings. The Lord of lords. He is the Alpha and Omega, the Author and the Finisher of our faith. To Him be the glory. To Him be the honor, forever and ever! Amen.

THE MOST PRECIOUS GIFT EVER GIVEN

The most precious gift that has been given to all believers, outside of the obvious gift of eternal life, is the gift that continually abides in us. I am talking about the Holy Spirit, and I do not mean in a Pentecostal or Charismatic sense alone. One of the things God holds very sacred, I believe most sacred concerning us, is our personal communion and relationship with Him; our oneness with Him. The place where we live by every word that proceeds from His mouth (Matthew 4:4). Where we live, move, and have our being in Him (Acts 17:28). Where we no longer live, and the life we now live is Christ (Galatians 2:20). The place where we do what we see Him do and say what we hear Him say (John 5:19, 12:49), because we are in love with Him. The place where His presence is the prize of our lives. The secret place that belongs to every believer, the place where we hear God speak for Himself—face to face, as a man speaks to a friend (Exodus 33:11).

This is crucial for us to understand, because everything God has designed will secure, empower, and purpose itself to create the platform necessary for this sacred communion to exist. Men have tried to get in between this sacred union and make themselves the voice of it. When they do this, they step on Holy Ground, in a dangerous way. "What God has joined together, let not man separate" (Mark 10:9).

Whatever this revival and reformation will look like, it will always focus its attention on the things God holds most sacred. For this reason, it is of the upmost importance to be mindful of the foundation we are building upon.

When revival manifests, and reformation and restoration take place, a few things will be obvious: The saints will experience more freedom, more empowerment, more grace, more love, more faith, more hope—not less of any of these things. They will bear more of the fruit of the Spirit. They will be more patient, more kind, more joyful, more loving, more peaceful, experiencing more goodness, and more faithful—not only within themselves, but in others they are built together with. Whatever revival, reformation, and restoration looks like, this will be the fruit of it.

Apostles, prophets, evangelists, pastors, and teachers are given to us by Christ for this very purpose, so that we will live by every word that proceeds from God's mouth, not their mouths. From Him (Christ), every joint will be supplied. That said, what we *should* hear from their mouths is what they have seen and heard from their experience with Christ. The apostle John said it well in this scripture:

> That which was from the beginning, which we have heard, which we have seen with our eyes, which we have looked at and our hands have touched—this we proclaim concerning the Word of life. ~ 1 John 1:1, NIV.

WE MUST BE IN LOVE

When I was born again on December 10, 1982, I experienced the unbelievably good and precious love of God. I was so happy and totally innocent in my heart concerning my experience. I was telling everyone who would listen what had happened to me. I was so excited at the prospect of joining with other believers, because surely they too were having the same experience as me. I thought to myself, *How wonderful it would be to join with others.*

Sadly, the more I shared what the Lord had done in my life, the madder some folks got. It got to the point where some would even lash out at me. I'm not talking about unbelievers, but brothers and sisters in Christ!

It seemed there were many times they were sorry to see me coming. This brought me so much confusion. I was told the "new" would wear off and God would put me down so I could learn to walk without this experience I was having. Then, I would grow up and settle down. Yet, as I studied the Scriptures, I realized that attitude that was being spewed over me was the very thing Jesus rebuked when He said, "Yet I hold this against you: You have forsaken the love you had at first" (Revelation 2:4).

While it is true that we grow up in Him, it is also true that we should be growing up in our first love, not departing from it. We learn to live in the innocence of His love that was poured out in our hearts. Later in life, I finally succumbed to the pressure and cares of this world. I became cynical and pessimistic. It took the strong hand of God to bring me back from this type of spiritual death. It cost me more than I could pay to revert back from the thinking He came to deliver me from to begin with, but He paid that price. I am thankful that I have learned, and I am still learning, that the price He paid is still paid in full.

These are some of the things I have learned: It was for freedom's sake that Christ came to set us free. He first called us to peace. Then, He taught us that all things are possible when we live in Him. He also taught us that favor with men does not equal favor with God. In fact, if that were the case, Jesus, Paul, Stephen, and the rest of the apostles of the Lamb failed, because they were all murdered. That's not the favor most of us are looking for or acknowledge.

It hurts to be rejected, to be forgotten. It hurts to come in last, but none of these things hurts as much as the pain of losing our first love. I don't want to grow up in anything else. One day the last will be first, the rejected will be received, and justice will prevail. (There is a promise also for those who have made themselves first in this life.) In all these things, we are more than conquerors. Our experience in this earth cannot take away our first love. This world cannot take away the love that comes from Christ. Even in this world He keeps us, and nothing can snatch His children from His grip. He loves us, and He is the prize we've been after all along.

To follow God requires one thing and one thing only: You must be in love with Him. You must be in love with Him whom you have encountered—not the *idea* of Him, nor what some *say* of Him. From this elevated place of being in love, we will hear His voice and live from every word that proceeds from His mouth.

Either we are following Him whom we have encountered and are in love with, or we are following what we think of the One in whom we once encountered. To do the latter is to have a relationship with our own reasoning. Doctrines of men always satisfy our own reasoning, which we have been instructed not to lean on (Proverbs 3:5). If we love the doctrine of Whom we once encountered above our love relationship with Whom we have encountered, we have lost our first love. We have then fallen to a place where we love being "right" intellectually and pointing out those who are "wrong." This satisfies the lust of our own intellect and our desire to elevate ourselves over others at the expense of their own well-being. To follow after doctrine over an encounter with the living God is to turn our backs on Life for the sake of looking right in the eyes of man.

To walk in love, you must be in love. To be in Christ is to be in Love. God is love, and since Jesus is God, then Love is our Cornerstone, and to be built upon Love we must first be in love.

THE INTELLECT

Seeing the obvious, it is very easy to know that the world's intellectual advances in technology, medicine, industry, communication and the like is truly astounding. That said, it is just as easy to see that our spiritual advancement is simultaneously taking a nose dive. With our great intellect, we have "thought" ourselves into the abyss. We have never been more polarized than we are today, both as individuals and as a people. It was our intellect that brought us to this place. We have no one to thank but ourselves for that, so hold your applause.

No matter how intellectually advanced we become, no matter how great our ability to reason, our intellect will never be able to answer spiritual, heart issues. That is not to say that intellect is not useful when it comes to communicating wisdom from an unseen realm, because it certainly is. However, intellect alone does not determine the heart that motivates it. If anything, I find that the smarter we seem to become, the faster we divide and separate to the point that we no longer recognize each other. We simply choose to ignore the possibility that we could be spiritually flawed, and the answer requires a greater reasoning than the reasoning we have. If what we see today is the result of how "wonderful" and "intelligent" we believe we are, we should be embarrassed, not patting ourselves on the back.

The latter rain of God's Spirit has begun (Joel 2:28, Acts 2:17, Haggai 2:9), but it will not be seen with the eyes of those who assume they see, but by the eyes of those who know they are blind without Jesus.

> At that time Jesus answered and said, "I thank You, Father, Lord of heaven and earth, that You have hidden these things from the wise and prudent and have revealed them to babes. ~ Matthew 11:25

A KEY TO HEARING GOD'S VOICE

As I mentioned in my testimony, I was in a horrible place when the Lord came and visited me on June 1, 2010. At this time, He began dialoguing with me more clearly than ever before, which has continued to this day. I want to share a key to hearing God's voice that has been given to me through this ongoing encounter.

Because of the mess I was in early on, I would always approach God in a petitioning manner. I was looking for answers to my issues. *How is this going to happen; how is that going to happen? What do I need to do here; what do I need to do there?* This was the way I would approach God, but He began showing me things that had nothing to do with my predicament. He was giving me answers to things I wasn't even asking for. This left me at a crossroads. *Did I want what I thought I needed, or did I want to hear His voice? Did I want to sit as His feet and hear what He had to say, or did I only want my questions answered?*

Part of following God means we trust Him above all else, which includes trusting that He will provide what we need when we need it. We must hear what He is saying, when He is speaking. It may seem, at times, as if God gives you volumes of revelation for *other* people with wisdom and clarity. Love enables us to be the messenger, even if it feels like we aren't receiving anything for ourselves. This does not come naturally to us, but it cultivates a sense of humility, faith, and trust in us that is beyond ourselves. When we seek Him first, the things we think are important will be added to us (Matthew 6:33).

Here is another thought: If God is not worried about those things, we don't have to concern ourselves with them, either. This alone should increase our faith and set us free. It's not that things that are important to us aren't important to God; everything that is important to us is important to God. However, when we obsessively worry over these things and repeatedly beg God to fix them, it often serves little to no purpose.

If something bothering you is seemingly unimportant to God at any given moment, don't allow it to occupy too much space in your head. This can be true with addictions, financial issues, sicknesses, depression, anxieties, or whatever. Sometimes, we have to reckon ourselves dead to what we don't know and alive to what we do know, trusting that God's grace is sufficient. Otherwise, we will shut down or squelch the building process God has started in us with our own fear, doubt, and unbelief. As I have followed God, the things I seemed to be fixated on and worried about at first had to become non-issues while God was speaking to me about other things. Over time, these things began to fall away and continue to fall away as if they were never even present in my mind.

This leads us to the final point. The last thing God spoke to me was, *Contend for my presence.*

You may have a big-picture revelation, and want big answers and resources to put what you see into effect. Surely, if it happened this way, you would build what you glimpsed with your own hands. This is often how a "house" ends up being built in vain. The initial vision may very well be from God, but you don't just need one word from God; you need God to actually build the house. This may happen through your hands, but there is a world of difference between God building the house and the house being established by human effort, wisdom, and reasoning.

The way ordained by the Lord, from the beginning, that will get you there the quickest, legitimately, and without sorrow, is to contend for His presence. You do this by fixing your eyes on Him, the Author and Finisher of your faith. There is only one legitimate way to enter into that which was finished, and that is through the "narrow gate," the very Son of God (Matthew 7:13-14; John 10:9).

God sent us His Spirit so we could have intimacy with Him and enter into His very presence. Our chief purpose in this life is to know God, and to respond to what we see Him say and do. This is what it means to "contend for His presence." Just as the followers of Jesus went into Pentecost as *disciples*, but came out of this experience as *apostles* of the Lamb. The presence of God changes us, which is why it must always hold a precedence in our lives, even above our gifts, callings, and ministries.

This is a key to reformation. When you turn this key, you have to be willing to walk away from life as you have previously known it, perhaps even the Christian life as you have understood it. I have made this choice and have not since regretted it even though God seems to only give me one piece of the puzzle at a time. Still, I continue to move forward, in faith, one step at a time.

THE ENEMY OF REFORMATION

Scripture shows us a major enemy of revival, reformation, and restoration, though it is easy to miss if you are not looking for it. This enemy is the *religious spirit*, which was commonly manifested by the Pharisees against Jesus.

The reason why Jesus was despised by the Pharisees was because He had not been working in *their* vineyards; He had not jumped through *their* hoops of worthiness. He didn't go through their schools or sit under their teachings. He didn't look, think, or act as they did; He lived in another realm entirely. He had an authority that did not originate from them; He showed up and began speaking with an authority He had not earned from them. He had a place at the table He didn't "deserve," and they were furious about it. He wasn't interested in their opinions or accolades, so, in their hearts, they decided He had to go. Their hearts were so filled with their own ideas about what God was like that they were driven to murder His Son.

Religious people want a revival where people "get what they deserve," while God wants people to receive what they don't deserve and what they could never earn. Sure, this requires repentance, but it doesn't require our approval. In fact, many are sure revival is coming because of what we believe we [as a people] deserve, but what we deserve has nothing to do with it. The prodigal son's older brother wasn't happy when his brother was restored with the ring and the robe. He was not happy when his father threw a party for his brother after what his brother had done. He wanted his brother to be put in the place that *he* believed he deserved; yet, his father had a different plan. The older brother wanted the younger to be placed in a servant's role, and the younger brother actually suggested this to the father, but this was not part of the father's heart or his agenda.

Revival dies quickly when those to which God sends with His word are seen as those who don't deserve to give it to others. When God raises up voices who show up in the last hour of the day, yet receive the same wage as those who have been toiling for years (Matthew 20:1-16). It is the hearts of those who worked in the vineyard all day that reject Christ when He shows up in the last hour without their approval. It is this offence God wants to remove from our hearts.

It is time we all get real about what is really in our hearts if we want to see revival come. If Jesus had given *any* of us what we deserved, nobody would be saved, and Jesus couldn't possibly deserve all the glory in the end.

No one deserved the healing they received. No one deserved their deliverance. It was God's grace alone that spoke otherwise. So, if you are looking for a revival that puts people in their place according to what you believe they deserve, you will be disappointed. The revival Jesus brings is the one we realize we have no part in other than to say "yes" to what He wants to do. He comes to restore the life He desires for us, and what we deserve has nothing to do with it. If any part of it is deserved, it's no longer by grace; it's an earned result. This doesn't mean we don't "count the cost." There is a cost we must count, a test we must pass: If we want to see revival, we need to prepare to see things that reveal what's really in our hearts, and we need to be willing to be delivered of such things.

THE ENEMY OF OUR SOULS

According to Jesus, the "thief" comes to steal, kill, and destroy (John 10:10). Any foundation the enemy has ever laid in the hearts of men has always led to theft, murder, death, and destruction. His tool belt always includes condemnation, seduction, intimidation, lies, manipulation, and control. He masquerades as an "angel of light" or a "seducer." However, he is nothing but an imposter, deceiving any and all that he can. He attempts to pervert our thoughts with situations that cause fear, doubt, and unbelief to grow in our hearts.

The enemy of our souls attempts to seduce us with our own desires by leading us to question what the Lord Himself speaks to our hearts. The lust of the eyes, the lust of the flesh, and the pride of life are the areas where he is able to infiltrate our souls (1 John 2:16). He renders his victims, helpless, hopeless, faithless, loveless and, ultimately, orphaned, because he is no father. Rather, he is a betrayer, a denier, and a deceiver in every form and shape that he emerges. He is the "accuser of the brethren" (Revelation 12:10).

Ode of the Enemy

Don't try to take my excuses away,
To plunder and pillage, to have my own way.
Keep pointing out slip ups, it's just what I need,
To continue my journey, my murderous spree.
Don't stop accusing, it's fuel for the fire,
To kill off another, to kill love's desire.
Don't stop the lying and backbiting please,

THE ENEMY OF OUR SOULS

It makes me legitimate, it makes them believe.
Don't stop the judgments, it makes me look pure,
To take down another who fights to endure.
Don't stop the greed, it runs men wild,
To abandon their families, to abandon a child.
Don't stop the mighty, they're making their mark.
They bully the weak, still trapped in the dark.
Don't stop the thinkers, elite in their ways,
Quoting some wisdom, birthed in a grave.
Don't stop the builders, a palace they build,
To express all the vanity, they couldn't conceal.
Don't stop the division, I need it to hide,
It gives me my method, to bring down the Bride.
So don't stop what you're doing; keep walking in pride,
The sky is the limit, with you on my side.

PERSONAL ACCOUNTS

The following are three personal accounts of God's work that I witnessed from 1999 through 2010. I believe these encounters reveal a taste of the things to come, which I have been describing throughout this book. These accounts also reveal how the enemy rises up in the midst of these moves of God as well. I will speak in more detail throughout this book concerning these things. Where the Spirit of the Lord [truly] is, there is liberty; however, everywhere Jesus went, devils manifested in the hearts of men. To be honest, these things can happen to and through any of us if we are weak, even when we are His children. When these kinds of things happen, they can be dealt with appropriately, just as Jesus did. The glory of God is coming and He is preparing us.

Years ago, around 1999, I caught a brief glimpse of God's work in a way I had not yet seen personally. I believe that what I saw and experienced points to what revival could look like, especially in the areas of harvest, empowerment, and the Lord's presence coming as a refiner's fire. Obviously, I am sure that God has moved this way in many places, but this particular experience was one that I personally witnessed.

It happened at a small Baptist church in Eastman, Georgia. The pastor invited us to come and do a "prayer and praise service" (as he called it), so that's what we did. His name was Gerald Conley. At the time, he was a Baptist pastor who had recently experienced the baptism of the Holy Spirit and wanted to see revival. Over the years, he has become one of my closest friends.

Christy and I sang and played songs and I would minister and speak in between songs. One night while we were there, I had just gotten through with a song when people began to stand up, one after another, and confess their sins. There was no altar call, no prodding, no calling folks out; we were just leading worship and talking about the need to repent from being so caught up in the wisdom of this age. Many were weeping, and I was shocked by what I was seeing. People were confessing things and lifestyles that would be shocking anywhere, but no one said a word in response; we were all caught in a sense of shock and awe. People were judging their own hearts, but no one could possibly condemn those who confessed for the workings that were going on within themselves.

Gerald told me he saw a cloud of glory descending over us. I knew that everything in the atmosphere had completely shifted. There was a holy awe and tangible presence of God in the room, and I don't think there was a soul there that night who could deny what a powerful moment it was.

The Lord Himself was arresting our hearts and His Spirit was all over us. People were being set free of the torment they were carrying. One woman, who was overweight, stood up and said, through tears, "I don't feel fat in this place." She had previously struggled a great deal with the way she looked and the judgement she felt in public. God was not only freeing people from the burdens of sin, but the shame they carried as well. While His presence was surely there on other nights, this one night was like no other.

After this moment was in full swing for a while, some of the people there who were known to be ministers, got a little more comfortable and began laying hands on people and praying over folks. This normally wouldn't have bothered me, but it felt as though the moment was being hijacked. I could feel a cold, wet, blanket coming over the place, as God's Spirit lifted. It was like men were taking advantage of the moment for their own gain. Gerald and I have talked about that night many times over the years.

Outside of the book of Acts and Pentecost, this Scripture describes the event I saw taking place:

> "I will send my messenger, who will prepare the way before me. Then suddenly the Lord you are seeking will come to his temple; the messenger of the covenant, whom you desire, will come," says the Lord Almighty.
>
> But who can endure the day of his coming? Who can stand when he appears? For he will be like a refiner's fire or a launderer's soap. He will sit as a refiner and purifier of silver; he will purify the Levites and refine them like gold and silver. Then the Lord will have men who will bring offerings in righteousness, and the offerings of Judah and Jerusalem will be acceptable to the Lord, as in days gone by, as in former years. ~ Malachi 3:1-4, NIV.

This next story took place a few months after the visitation I had from the Lord on June 1, 2010. I was playing with the worship team at our home church, when I sensed a spiritual shift in the room. I began to minister from my heart to the people as the presence of God filled the room. People came to the altar on their own, and a strange thing began to happen. On the right side of the platform, everyone was weeping and some were wailing, as if some sort of deep intercession had come upon them. On the left side of the platform, everyone was laughing and some hysterically joyful. It was the strangest sight. I was simply testifying of what the Lord was speaking to my heart, and the next thing I knew, this was happening. The Lord moved suddenly.

With this description firmly planted, some other things happened as well. The senior leader came up to me and said, "You are probably going to get credit for this." He didn't seem to be very happy about it. Shortly after that service, the worship leader and her husband, who was also an elder in the church, stepped down citing the need to take a sabbatical. I remember she was not very happy in that moment, either. Whatever it was that took place, I knew it would not be long before it ended, because the leadership of the church seemed to have rejected it while it was still

PERSONAL ACCOUNTS

in process. Sometimes, it can also be the messenger who is rejected. Were these bad people? No way! I still share a closeness and love with them. They are simply people, just like the rest of us. I don't fully comprehend or know why they reacted the way they did or what was going on within them, but I do know the enemy is relentless to sow destruction wherever he can.

I do not always know when God will move in the manner He did in this church, and I am not sure how it will look each time. However, I have become familiar with the things that tend to rise up in an attempt to stop God's work—jealousy, envy, and pride. The Lord may move among us, but if our hearts are not in a good place, we will reject it.

I am not going to say that this account was a glimpse of revival, because, in reality, it was too short lived. Because of the events that transpired, we will never know for sure. However, I believe it was a glimpse of what "not to do" when the Lord begins to move over His people. We all cry out for revival, but more often than not, it is something in our own hearts that rises up against it. I can't hold these actions against these individuals, as I have done the same things myself, as you will read in the next story.

This story took place before my encounter with the Lord in June of 2010. My wife had been attending a conference over the weekend where God had touched many, leaving them filled with hope. A well-known minister was speaking on the final night, and she wanted me to attend. I was suffering from depression at the time, and had little desire to attend. At the same time, I did not want to disappoint my wife, so I reluctantly went to the service with little to no expectation.

When the minister got up to speak, holy laughter began to break out across the room. I'll confess, the more everyone laughed, the angrier I became. After a while, the minister decided there was no use in trying to speak, and instead opted to form a "fire tunnel." (This is where people form two lines, facing one another, and lay hands on folks for the purpose of blessing and impartation as they pass from one end of the 'tunnel' to the other.)

I was struggling with depression and desperately needed joy; yet the joy of those present became the catalyst for the rage I felt within, because I hardened my heart. Now, I could say that they were just out of order with all that happiness, but does that really make sense? Rather than embracing the possibility that God may touch me in this way, thus delivering me, I was happier holding on to my anger and depression in some sort of self-righteous posture.

It is these types of strongholds within us that hinder and reject the work of God in our lives. To be clear, there are things that happen at times that are indeed *not* of God. However, I have found that much of the time when we reject something it is because we are worshipping our own thoughts of what we believe about God, when God is standing right in front of us. Isn't this the very reason the Pharisees couldn't recognize Jesus, while prostitutes and tax-collectors could?

Was there any fallout to my rejecting this work of God? Yes, perhaps more than I may ever know. Hard-hearted disobedience will always cost us more than we want to pay. Thankfully, we serve a long-suffering God who is full of grace, mercy, and patience. God is love, and love recognizes when we don't know what we are doing and forgives us, because Jesus paid the debt for our ignorance and disobedience once and for all.

PROPHETIC WORDS OF REVIVAL, REFORMATION, AND RESTORATION

The next section of this book contains prophetic words I have received from the Lord through times of prayer, where I simply listened to hear His voice. These words are specifically relevant to the current season the Church is in concerning revival, reformation, and restoration. These words also acted as a catalyst for the birthing of this book.

The Passing of Billy Graham — February 2018

It has been prophesied more than once of a great global harvest that would begin and have no ebb until the return of Christ. This will come through a great awakening. Some call it revival, a move of God—you can frame it how you want; nevertheless, a surge of new believers will be harvested before the return of the Lord, accompanied by the Holy Spirit moving mightily through His people with signs and wonders.

Though this has already begun, the evangelistic mantle must be picked up and wielded in the power of the Spirit for this to happen in its fullness. With the passing of Billy Graham, this mantle has been surely cast down at our feet to be picked up for this moment.

How do I know this to be true? Consider this Scripture:

> "Most assuredly, I say to you, unless a grain of wheat falls into the ground and dies, it remains alone; but if it dies, it produces much grain." ~ John 12:24

I was pondering these things yesterday, when I believe the Lord spoke to me saying, *This wave of revival will be accompanied by another great and final point of reformation.* He then began to help "think me through" the reformation that occurred in the 1500s when Martin Luther wrote the 95 Thesis, in which he proclaimed that we receive salvation by grace through faith. The Catholic Church at that time was raising money by selling indulgences for the right to receive blessing from the Church. Indulgences were granted for the temporary lessening of punishment for sins. Also at that time, as I've been taught, only ministers were approved to read Scripture because they believed they were the only ones who could properly interpret it for others. Martin Luther protested this idea and, due to the invention of the printing press, quickly went to work putting the Bible into print in common language and into the hands of all who believed. Thus, the Protestant Reformation was born.

The reformation of this hour will be concerning the Holy Spirit's involvement with every believer, and the fact that God is raising up a generation who will live by every word that proceeds from His mouth, where we are indeed a people who live, move, and have our being in Him, doing what we see Him do and seeing what we hear Him say. A people who accept the fact that they no longer live, and that the life they now live is Christ. A people in whom we see the fruition of Ephesians 4:

> From him the whole body, joined and held together by every supporting ligament, grows and builds itself up in love, as each part does its work. - Ephesians 4:16, NIV.

Apostles, prophets, evangelists, pastors, and teachers, equip the body so that "From Him"—the head of the Church—each member will flow. Not from themselves, but from Him (Christ), the head of the Church. The five-fold ministries are not the government of Christ exclusively. While they do play an essential role, everyone who is in Christ is, at the very least, an ambassador endowed with gifts and callings, and empowered by the Holy Spirit. Therefore, all who are in Christ represent His government, of which there will be no end. Apostles and prophets lay the foundation, but the foundation they lay will always point to the reality that those in whom they impart foundation to are to live themselves by every word that proceeds from the mouth of God. This is the point of this final reformation, which is actually a restoration to what was present in the early Church. The reason it will appear more as a "reformation" than a "restoration," is because, over the last few centuries, we have drifted far away from the original design of God. Yet, He has preserved His Church through the ages.

When Martin Luther set out on a quest to put the word of God in every believer's hand, the clergy became nervous. In the same way, when every believer begins to understand that they themselves are to live by every word that comes from the mouth of God, don't think for a moment today's religious clergy won't get just as nervous as their forefathers.

Five-fold ministry, by the leading of the Holy Spirit, is designed by Jesus to equip us who believe to live by every word that proceeds from the mouth of God. However, unless the Lord builds the house, the house is built in vain.

June 1st 2010, I had a visitation from the Lord where He said, *Men get a glimpse of what I want to do in the earth, then they try to build it with their hands.* So, while we are indeed tracking correctly in recognizing our need for the five-fold ministry, we have tried to implement this ministry with our own reasoning, strength, and power. We have become nothing more than what already existed, though with different titles. Now, we sell apostolic "coverings" instead of indulgences, but for the same purpose of raising funds. This is not good! (It should be noted that not all who hold these offices are in any way doing this, though some are.)

We have gotten to the place where we believe that only those in five-fold ministry are capable to actually live by every word that proceeds from the mouth of God; when, in fact, every saint may do this. It is the duty of those in ministry to equip the saints for this very reason.

When the writer of Hebrews declared that Jesus is the "Author and Finisher" of our faith, he wasn't kidding. To believe that this change would be dangerous only reveals our doubt that Jesus is able to finish in all of us what He began. While apostles and prophets lay foundations in our lives to equip us, they are neither the Author or the Finisher—Jesus is.

Years ago, Bill Hamon referred to this day as the "Saints Movement," and this revelation continues to become clearer.

The last word the Lord spoke to me during the 2010 visitation was, *Contend for My presence.* As I've said before, the only thing that has ever changed anyone is an encounter with Jesus. We need to stay on the pilgrimage of being effectively engaged with His presence. We not only need to encounter Christ regularly; I believe we are going to see His people go into the secret place and never come out again! They will give from this place of victory. Then, Heaven indeed invades our lives here on earth. Be blessed! There are great days ahead.

> Set your mind on things above, not on things on the earth. For you died, and your life is hidden with Christ in God. When Christ who is our life appears, then you also will appear with Him in glory. ~ Colossians 3:2-4

Revival with No Ebb — March 4, 2018

In the 1930s, there was a word given to a group of men of a final revival that was coming in which there would be no end. Arthur Burt, from the United Kingdom, was one of those men. During this period, Arthur Burt travelled with Smith Wigglesworth, and these two experienced an astonishing outpouring of healing, signs, and wonders. For years, Arthur was the only one living that actually witnessed hearing that word.

Bob Jones was another from the United States who had received this same type of word. At the time, the two had no knowledge of each other. From all accounts, Bob Jones believed he would see the beginning of this move before he died. In the late 1980s Bob Jones felt he was supposed to encourage a man in Great Britain. Rev. Steve Scroggs, in *The Awakening of the Lord's End of Days*, gave this account:

One morning in the late 1980s, when Bob was praying and talking to God, the Lord told Bob that he wanted him to encourage one of his men in Great Britain. The Lord said, *In the year you were born I gave him a word, and he has not seen this word fulfilled. Tell him that he will see this word come to pass before he dies.*

The way I understand it, Bob Jones told this word to someone who had just returned from England. Bob told them they had just been at this man's house, and they shared that they had just visited Arthur Burt. From all accounts, this word meant a lot to Arthur. Just a couple of years ago, both men passed away. Arthur Burt was 102. I was riding down the highway on March 4, 2018, when I believe the Lord spoke this to my heart:

This revival with no intended end has started, yet there is a key and a warning that must be heard. The keys to this revival are the combined messages of the two prophets who carried this prophetic word. Bob Jones was asked, and he asked, "Did you learn to love?" Arthur Burt brought a deeper insight of humility. Those two men were marked by these words. My church must walk in both, with the wisdom of both revelations firmly planted. It is the combination of love and humility that will keep legs under this movement.

Love and humility are defined by human standards, but, in reality, are actually the synonymous winds that define the essence of Love Himself. These are two keys to the Kingdom that must be found. The knowledge of Kingdom keys does not equal the effective possession for their use. To turn these keys requires transformation from the wisdom of these keys. If this doesn't happen, then this generation could repeat what every generation before it has.

When My Spirit moves, the mistake of the previous generation has historically been entering into elitism. Elitism is neither love nor humility, and My Glory will not rest on the snobbery of men. Once the people who receive a move of My Spirit enters into elitism, they will quickly become an irrelevant wineskin of what once was that the next generation will soon scoff at. Do not scoff at the previous generations or walk prideful in the knowledge of the things known or things to come. If you have already done this, you have already begun to step into elitism. Turn away from that heart condition, and don't be captured by it again. To eat from the Tree of Life requires the understanding of grace.

A true revelation of My grace gives no man any reason to boast. Everything man has was given to Him. Therefore, seek out and ask for the wisdom of these instructions and there will indeed be no end!

The Generation of Restoration — January 30, 2015

In this hour, God has been raising up a generation who does what they see Jesus do and says what they hear Him say. God is raising a generation whose intimacy with Christ is growing and has grown to such a place where they literally live by every word that comes from the mouth of God. When this happens at the high level described in Ephesians, the Lord Himself will indeed be building His temple at a much quicker pace.

Pharaohs have always built pyramid systems off the backs of those in whom they enslave. Jesus will build His temple by the power of His Spirit through freed men who have been born of God.

While those called to be Apostles and Prophets are part of the building process, they are neither the Author or the Finisher of your faith—Jesus is. Unless the Spirit builds the house, the house is built in vain.

While it is vital that we have true five-fold ministry, parts of it should not be elevated to the place it has become with some, and other parts must be raised. They should think highly of themselves, but not more highly than they ought.

When I was naked, the apostolic networks didn't cover me. When I was hungry, they didn't feed me. When I was imprisoned, they didn't visit me. I wrote to them and I tried to connect, but they didn't respond.

However, when I was naked Jesus covered me. When I was hungry, Jesus fed me. When I was imprisoned, Jesus visited me, and he lifted me up and set me on higher ground, and when I began to testify of His goodness, of what He did for me, and I began to do what I saw Him do and say what I heard Him say, they finally showed up, and they seemed a bit angry. They asked me, "Who gave you the authority to speak in Jesus name?" They asked me, "Who is your covering?"

PROPHETIC WORDS OF REVIVAL, REFORMATION, AND RESTORATION

My response is this: What I have cannot be given by you, it's not yours to give, and what I have cannot be taken by you, it's not yours to take, and so it is with all of whom the Lord has called and sent.

True Apostles and Prophets will always be pointing to Jesus with all authority—with mighty authority. They won't settle for pointing to their own authority, or the authority of their networks and associations. They will not point to the approval that comes through men but will reveal the authority that comes from the very breath of God. They will not see their networks as the goal, but as a catalyst for God's beloved bride.

Keys, Open Doors, Prison Breaks, Recompense, Reformation, and Restoration — February 23, 2018

My daughter, Tessa, has a Toyota Prius. Not long ago, the battery went dead, so we had to take her to work. While she was gone, Christy took her key fob and tried to open the car door, but since the battery was dead the keyless entry device didn't work, either. Since neither of us was familiar with this type of device, we didn't even know how to get into the car. Christy began to do some research on the Internet and discovered that the fob had a hidden key inside. When she figured out how to get the key to emerge, she was able to get into the car, where she found that a small, overhead light had been left on. She turned off the light, popped the hood, and was able to jump start the car. Afterward, she said to me, "I can't help but think this is some sort of prophetic picture."

She was so right.

On Wednesday evening, February 14, 2018, a prophet by the name of Jeff Jansen came to Ramp Church. After a long period of ministry, he called us all to come near the platform. While he was ministering, he turned and looked toward me, then he made a motion of sticking a key into my belly and turning it. Somehow, in my Spirit, I knew it was the key of David, which held great personal significance to me.

Jeff later gave me an astounding prophetic word regarding my future, as was witnessed and followed by a prophetic word from Karen Wheaton. Since that night, an encounter and profound impartation I had from the

Lord in 1997 began to stir and emerge from within. Something in my heart was unlocked when he shoved the "key" into my stomach. I told Christy that I felt like the Lord, through the obedience of Jeff Jansen, got an old car (me) cranked and installed a supercharger in the engine! The prophet possessed a key that needed to be turned in me for the purposes of the Lord to be fulfilled.

This takes us to the next part of what I have been seeing. Right now, in the Spirit, there are hidden keys that are to be discovered quickly, because there are doors that must be opened. These hidden keys will be able to unlock doors in the Spirit realm that those in their sphere of influence need to go through.

Just a few days ago, I had a vision where I saw many folks standing in a large hallway that had doors on both the right and left. Somehow, I knew the people who were in the hall had already passed through the doors on the left. They also knew that they needed to pass through the doors on the right to continue on their journey. There were people standing behind the doors on the left, knocking and waiting to be let out. However, the people in the hall were so focused on getting through the doors on the right that they ignored them.

Then the Lord spoke to me, saying, *The people in the hall have keys to open the doors on the left that would enable those behind the doors to come out. When they open these doors on the left, those behind them possess the keys that will enable all to go through the doors on the right, which those presently in the hallway do not possess. When some of those people in the hall realize that those who are ready behind the doors on the left hold the keys to the doors on the right that they wish to enter, they will begin to release them so all can continue on their journey with speed and increase.*

I didn't quickly share this vision, because I felt there was more to glean. While meditating on the vision in the wee hours of the morning, I believe the Lord spoke to me and said there were seven doors on the right, which represented seven spheres of influence. The people in the hallway were ministers, businessmen, statesmen, scientists, entertainers, educators, family members, media folks, and artists who were established leaders in their respected fields. The doors on the right represented further breakthrough into those spheres of influence. The thought very much resembled Lance Wallnau's *Seven Mountain Mandate teaching*, for those who are familiar.

When meditating on the reason for the hold-up, I felt the Lord began to say, *Reformation is coming—reformation is here. It is hardly welcomed, and only those who hear what the Spirit is saying will initially respond, though others will follow their response. Some of them still have the remnants of fear, doubt, hurt, unforgiveness, insecurity, control and the like, working in them that would blind them in this moment, but who can control Me?*

Those behind the doors on the left hold the keys of reformation that will raise a generation as I have raised these hidden ones to see Me and to hear Me. They will speak as I speak, they will walk as I walk. They will bind and they will loose. They will not love their lives even unto death. These are my mighty ones, humbled by My hand, waiting to be revealed for this moment in time. Many of these have already been through what some of those who are presently ahead of them would have quit had they been faced with the same trials long ago. These are those who were despised, crushed, betrayed, written off, and forgotten. Those with chains binding them tightly and weighing them down but they kept going anyway—they did not quit—they would not quit. Those mighty ones who are not for sale—no they will not be bought. Those who made up their minds to serve Me in the midst of undo suffering, temptations, and calamity, who said, 'If things never change, I will still serve my Father.'

Those who know they have nothing that wasn't given to them. Those who will know and say, 'The only leg they have to stand on is Jesus and Him crucified.'

These are the same who were raised in the pits and prisons of affliction, and bear the scars of My sufferings. These are My dreaded ones who I Myself have raised, and they know no Father to themselves but Me.

They will say as Joseph said to his brothers, 'So then, it wasn't you who sent me here. It was God.'

These are my reformers, and today is their day of justice and recompense.

They will walk in the Spirit of Elijah who will restore all things. They will turn the hearts of the fathers to the children, and the hearts of the children to the fathers. These are those who live to hear My voice.

Some of those ahead of them that I have called according to My purposes will know them and begin to release them into the place that I have called them to. They were sent ahead of them, even for this purpose. Yet, as those who are being released through those doors they themselves will open the doors for their peers who are still behind the other doors, similar to a prison break. Therefore, I say loose the bound mighty ones who I have sent to do My will. My relentless ones whose very presence—My presence—strikes fear in the hearts of men and devils. Yes, My dreaded ones that all creation groans for, and hell trembles at their sight. I will reform and restore My Church yet again through these mighty ones. Let this word be an enabling key being purposely turned for this moment!

Amen! It's time to enter through the doors of reformation and harvest. These are the days of Elijah, so prepare the way of the Lord! Make straight in the desert a highway for our God! As Isaiah prophesied and Jesus proclaimed two thousand years ago, let this be what we proclaim as well:

> "The Spirit of the Lord is upon Me, because He has anointed Me to preach the gospel to the poor; He has sent Me to heal the brokenhearted, to proclaim liberty to the captives and recovery of sight to the blind, to set at liberty those who are oppressed; to proclaim the acceptable year of the Lord." ~ Luke 4:18-19

A Word to All who are Called by My Name — March 11, 2018

I love all races—white, black, Asian, Arab, Native American—all races of every kind. I love many of the cultural aspects that come from every race. However, what I do hate is ideologies that exalt themselves above the truth of who I AM. I hate the "isms" that exhalt themselves above who IS. Every "ism" that exalts itself above who I AM is fueled by the spirit of the antichrist, no matter what color face is put upon it.

PROPHETIC WORDS OF REVIVAL, REFORMATION, AND RESTORATION

So many who say they are Mine, who truly may be, are waiting for My return in hopes that I will validate them so they can say, "I told you so!" Yet when I return, they will not be able to utter such words. For if they are Mine they will do what my servant Joshua did when confronted by the commander of the army. If you can get this, you and your household will be blessed. If you do not get this, it is time to weep between porch and altar until you do.

Now when Joshua was near Jericho, he looked up and saw a man standing in front of him with a drawn sword in his hand. Joshua went up to him and asked, "Are you for us or for our enemies?"

"Neither," he replied, "but as commander of the army of the Lord I have now come." Then Joshua fell facedown to the ground in reverence, and asked him, "What message does my Lord have for his servant?" ~ Joshua 5:13-14, NIV.

This will always be the proper response of those who follow Me. I wouldn't be giving you this word if it wasn't absolutely important at this moment. My sheep hear My voice, and respond accordingly. Hear Me this day, and know that I AM speaking what pleases Me to speak at this hour in time. You are My beloved, and I am no longer hiding who I AM from My beloved. You have entered into a new season, and know that I AM is with you. Have the heart of my servant Joshua as you enter into this place.

At this moment, lines are being drawn in the sand, not for My glory, but the glory of the reasoning of man. Not for my glory, but the glory of their own reasoning, so they can pat themselves on the back. They have totally given themselves over to the tree of the knowledge of good and evil. They worship themselves not Me. They do this in their own name, not Mine, yet they pretend to speak for Me. Very few are eating from the tree of life. Like walking graves, they come into agreement and eat from the source of death and proclaim the righteousness of it. They themselves are deceived.

Therefore, remove yourselves from this thinking, and devote yourselves to every word that proceeds from My mouth. Now is your time to be and to demonstrate all of who I AM to you.

KEYS TO REVIVAL

This next section contains a collection of revelatory keys that I believe are pertinent for this moment, keys designed to unlock the heart of God inside of us. These keys are designed to unlock those gifts and callings on a foundation that prepares us and enables us to overcome the enemies of our souls, as well as the enemies of restoration and revival.

I believe, and will always believe, that there is a remnant in every church that desires to follow Jesus with all their hearts. They know there is "more," but don't always know exactly how to get there. God is revealing gifts and callings within them. As they follow Him, these things will be revealed.

Once you have said, "Send me Lord; I will do anything!", watch out! You have given God permission to have His way in your life. This is the best decision a man or woman can make.

I am excited about God's ability to break through what cannot be broken through, to redeem the unredeemable, to heal the impossible, to restore the irreparable, to resurrect the buried, to restore sight to the blind. Jesus is Lord, and His Lordship holds no rivals.

MARY AND MARTHA

Twice a day, I try to spend time by myself where I position myself to allow the Spirit of the Lord to shape my thinking to what He is saying. Some of these moments have been the most fulfilling moments I have ever experienced in my life. Other times, it can be a battle where I am faced with extraordinary circumstances where if God doesn't show up, I'll be in trouble. However, God always responds.

Both this morning and this afternoon, I felt the Lord speaking to me through the story of Mary and Martha.

> Now it happened as they went that He entered a certain village; and a certain woman named Martha welcomed Him into her house. And she had a sister called Mary, who also sat at Jesus' feet and heard His word. But Martha was distracted with much serving, and she approached Him and said, "Lord, do You not care that my sister has left me to serve alone? Therefore tell her to help me."
>
> And Jesus answered and said to her, "Martha, Martha, you are worried and troubled about many things. But one thing is needed, and Mary has chosen that good part, which will not be taken away from her." ~ Luke 10:38-42

Most of us have heard this Scripture many times, but the Lord highlighted some things to me today that went deeper than what I had seen in times past. I have most often heard that we need both Mary and Martha to get things done, but after today, this notion has been challenged in me.

As a family, we have been in a place for an extended period of time where we set out to follow God with all of our hearts. To go where we believed He was sending us and to say what we believed He would have us say. To do this, we were faced with making choices that go against a lot of the wisdom and work ethics that we were raised with, and, to be honest, have been deeply steeped in. Obviously, a heart willing to sacrifice and to serve is a good thing, and I applaud that kind of heart in everyone. However, when it comes to following Jesus, there is something articulated in this Scripture that reveals a better way.

The Scripture says that Martha opened her home to Jesus, but chose to be distracted by what she perceived needed to be done. It is obvious that she had a chip on her shoulder because her sister was sitting at Jesus' feet while she was doing all the work. Yet, Jesus told her that Mary had chosen what was better.

Here's a point to consider: Mary had to choose to go against her cultural reasoning to make the decision to sit at Jesus' feet. She had to have known that her choice could anger those who witnessed her decision to draw from Jesus; yet, she knew in her heart that there would be more imparted into her in that moment than she may receive elsewhere in an entire lifetime. She chose to let nothing come between her and the Lord. Indeed, she chose that which was better. And perhaps, later on, Mary would have helped Martha serve those who were there.

I mentioned earlier that God is raising up a generation who will go into the secret place of His presence and never come out again. That is the choice that Mary was making. To sit at the feet of Jesus will challenge the cultural wisdom of the age we live in. Jesus is calling us to make the better choice. It may not be easy, but if it were, everyone would likely be doing it.

Jesus Himself said that His yoke was easy and His burden is light. I would go further to say that what makes making this choice seem so heavy is the scrutiny of what men think, and the scrutiny of doubt and unbelief that tries to impose itself in our thinking. When these things have no hold on us, the burden is as light as we will ever experience. In fact, the yoke and burden we were not created to carry is the load that comes from the evil wisdom of this age.

When you say "yes" to the better choice, you have actually chosen to forego the wisdom of men. We have become so gripped by the wisdom of this age, even our praying and fasting can cause us to miss Jesus when He comes, just as the Pharisees failed to recognize Him for who He was. Some churches have been built on the wisdom of Martha, when God has said that unless the Lord builds the house, the house is built in vain.

I am very aware that many of you have a great deal of tasks that must be accomplished every day, to the point that what I am suggesting may seem impossible. I understand how this goes, especially for those who are parents of young children. I have experienced this many times myself! However, God does not ask of us that which is impossible, because with God, all things are possible. Ask Him to show you what you can do where you are, with the responsibilities you have, and be willing to re-arrange your life as He may lead. Remember, He will equip you to do whatever He asks of you, and you will not be disappointed when you choose to follow His leading.

The place God is calling His Church to will require us to make the better choice, as Mary did. This Church lives by every word that proceeds from the mouth of God. It lives, moves, and has its being in Him. It does what it sees the Father do, and says what it hears Him say. It will be known as, *The House that Jesus built.*

God is pleased with us when we believe and receive what He did for us, but when we make the choice Mary did, God is "well pleased." He is raising up a generation who will go into the secret place of His presence and never come out again.

HE LOVES YOU ABOVE YOUR ABILITIES

What does this mean, that God "loves us above our abilities"? It means it is *you that* God wants—your heart and your affection. Before you are anything else, you are His child. Gifts and callings are a framework of expression to others, but without God's abiding presence in and over our personal lives, our gifts and callings will have little to no effect to others. After all, did He not love us when we were yet sinners?

When it comes to growing up in Christ, there are two things going on in the life of every believer, which sometimes happen simultaneously. At times, we are acutely aware of these things; other times, we are not aware at all. When we are first born again, and our spiritual lightbulb has gone off, we know that we know something has changed in our hearts. We have essentially transitioned from death to life. So, the first thing that happens is the knowledge that we are maturing. We are now babes in Christ. 1 John 2:12-14 references our progression as we grow. We are referred to as babes, little children, young men, and, finally, fathers. Obviously, this is not gender-specific, because in Christ there is no more male or female (Galatians 3:28). Do women not have to mature as well? Of course; we all do. And we mature in stages.

During this maturation in Christ, we are learning the basic principles of the doctrines of Christ, which are outlined in Hebrews 5:12 through Hebrews 6:3. (I am not going to expound on these things in this book, so you may desire to study these Scriptures on your own.) We learn about the baptism of the Holy Spirit. We begin to experience and hear the Lord's voice speaking to our hearts. We get acquainted with God's presence, both individually and corporately. We learn to become more discerning. You get the idea.

The second thing that happens, usually after a period of time where we grow up in Christ, we begin to discover our emerging gifts and callings. I say "usually," because I have seen what some folks are called to even before they were born again. Their calling is already at work, though the purpose is misappropriated.

While our gifts and callings are important to God, and given to us by Him, He loves us first and foremost because we are His sons and daughters. This is an absolute expression of a good father's love. Otherwise, God's love would be based on what we have to offer, and nothing could be further from the truth. We would do well to learn this.

We often love someone for what the person offers and the benefits they possess for us rather than the fact we should love simply for the sake of love, regardless of what they bring to us personally. When we get to the place that we can love in this way, a father or mother's heart is emerging within us.

As we go through the various stages of growing in Christ and discovering our gifts and callings, we will learn that the greatest discovery is that we are more valuable to God than what we can do for Him. May we hold the same value for God Himself as well.

Growing Up in Christ

God is raising up a generation who will live by every word that proceeds from His mouth. This implies a present-tense relationship. Every word that comes to us in the here and now from a living God who is capable of speaking for Himself to us. Jesus is the head of the Church, and He has called us to live, move, and have our being in Him.

> But He answered and said, "It is written, 'Man shall not live by bread alone, but by every word that proceeds from the mouth of God.'" ~ Matthew 4:4

All ministry is built on our individual life in Christ as a believer. It does not matter what we are called to if we as individuals do not live to do what we see Him do and say what we hear Him say. Because everything we are comes from this reality. If you have a prophetic or apostolic mantle without a father's heart, you will be more dangerous than good and leave a trail of casualties in your wake. It is more important that you possess the heart of the Father than it is that you have power and authority, because this will cause you to love others as God loves them.

This doesn't mean that an up-and-coming apostolic or prophetic voice cannot function in meetings, but if their hearts are turned to God, they will yield to a father or mother in the Spirit if they have one. The truth is, most of us don't do a very good job in this area. Being a father of nine children, some of whom are grown, I have learned that a lot of what I do involves tolerating ideas and ways of thinking that I know they will grow out of in time. Isn't that what our Father in Heaven has been doing for all of us from the beginning?

I remember watching westerns when I was a kid. In my generation, that was what we did. The same scenario would play out in most of these films—a conflict between the cowboys and the Indians. The young braves were always itching to go to war and demonstrate their manhood. They were not afraid of death. Without fail, the older chief would try to talk some sense into them. More often than not, the younger braves would run out prematurely and be routed by their enemy, or they would go too far in their anger and bring harsher judgement on themselves and their people. This happens often in the body of Christ as well.

The apostle Paul never said there were too many orphans; he said there were not many fathers. Fathers value their children more for who they are than what they can do for them. You are more valuable to God than your gifts and calling. Never lose sight of that.

You may have discovered you have an apostolic anointing and have great revelation concerning that gifting, but this doesn't mean you are automatically a father in the Spirit. A sixteen-year-old may have a driver's license and own a car, but the chances are high that he will not drive in the same manner as a fifty-year-old dad with a car full of children, whose love for his children will dictate the way he drives. I hope you can see where I am going with this, because the same is true for any office of ministry. All functions of ministry will operate at their fullest potential when the one who is gifted has a father's heart. This is not a matter of age or gender, but a matter of heart. It is also true that you can be a father in the Spirit and not be called to be in an office of ministry at all. We are all called to the ministry of reconciliation (2 Corinthians 5:18), and we should therefore all minister to each other and those who are lost.

If you are looking for a perfect person who never makes mistakes, you will never find one. Everyone who is called to ministry will go too far, say too much, put the cart before the horse, jump out too quickly, say the wrong thing at the wrong time, have a bad day—you name it and it will happen. However, one with a father's heart will get back up and face the music. He has learned he can't give up, no matter how tempting it can be to do so. Instead, he must return to his role as a father (or mother). It is the inescapable burden that love will not let go of. It is not one's gifts or calling that keeps them going; it is their love. We must learn to love.

Apostles are called to be "master builders" (1 Corinthians 3:10) in the building process of the Temple of the Lord—a temple not built by the hands of men, but by the Spirit of the living God.

MOTHERS AND FATHERS

Sometimes we have to give to others what we know they themselves will never give to us. Parents should know this really well. With our children, not only will they not give back some of the things we have given them, they should not be required to—not to us, anyway. What parent raises a child so the child will take care of them from that point on? Parents lay down their lives for their children, not children for the parents.

Sons and daughters need mothers and fathers. Gifts and callings are secondary; it is the paternal and maternal love that sons and daughters need most. Fathers and mothers value their children regardless of what manner of child they have. Whether their child is a scholastic genius, a world-class athlete, or whether they have Down syndrome, parents will love their children. If they don't, they are not truly functioning as mothers and fathers.

When a young soldier lies wounded and dying on the battlefield, he doesn't need a drill sergeant; he needs a father or mother's hand upon him, or even an empathetic brother's hand. He needs to be comforted. He needs assurance.

Years ago, when I was much younger, I was a deputy sheriff in southern Georgia. I did my best to leave the "deputy" in my patrol car when I came home from work, but I wasn't always successful in doing so. I had two little girls at the time who had no need for a deputy sheriff, and the presence of this demeanor in the lives of innocent little girls would have been detrimental to their health. What they really needed was a father. What sons and daughters need are mothers and fathers.

MOTHERS AND FATHERS

It has been said, "Only apostles can raise apostles," but I don't believe this is true. Billy Graham's daddy was a dairy farmer. And how smart were Albert Einstein's parents? I think you will find that almost every high achiever in history had regular, everyday parents, and some of them didn't have parents at all. While I'm sure they had role models and folks who held significance in their lives, there were no parents cloning themselves as "the next generation of greatness." I believe God is bigger than our thinking on this subject, and we must rethink our models for ministry that are born more of human reasoning than God's Spirit.

This does not mean that apostolic and prophetic sons and daughters will not profit from the mentorship of others who are ahead of them. I am not trying to reduce or take away from the roles of those called to the five-fold ministry. I am simply saying it is the father or mother's *heart* that qualifies them as physical or spiritual parents. A parent will stay with you through thick and thin when an apostle or prophet may not, and I believe the love of a father or mother is all that is needed to birth sons and daughters into their divine destinies. Mary and Joseph were not Messiahs, but they raised one. Elizabeth was not the forerunner, but she raised one. Jacob wasn't the prime minister of Egypt, but he raised one. Unless the Lord builds the house, the house is built in vain.

> Even if you had ten thousand guardians in Christ, you do not have many fathers, for in Christ Jesus I became your father through the gospel. ~ 1 Corinthians 4:15, NIV.

As I said earlier, Paul didn't say that there were "too many orphans;" he said there "weren't many fathers." You will also notice he didn't say there "aren't many apostles," and he specifically stated they had plenty of teachers instructing and guarding the truth. (Where the NIV uses the word "guardian," the NKJV and other translations use the word "instructor.") As the title of this section would indicate, mothers and fathers in the Spirit are needed in these times as perhaps never before. Not everyone has this level of spiritual influence in their lives, even if they are regular churchgoers. However, God Himself will intervene for anyone in this predicament, and will reveal Himself as a loving Father who has His children's best interest at heart.

God fathers all of us on some level, and He expects us to mature as fathers and mothers to others. He desires that there be fathers and mothers to protect and lead those who need this influence in their lives. Gifts and callings determine roles, but our hearts determine the depth and effect of the role we have in our fellowship with each other. The best "ministry" is built on the foundation of our personal relationship with Christ, as we learn from each stage of our growth in Him.

To be orphaned is to be left abandoned, either through the death of parents or their absence. I have heard leaders talk with disdain about those who possess an "orphan spirit," as if it is their own fault and responsibility to find someone to father their hearts. When Malachi 4 describes the Spirit of Elijah's coming, he states that it is the hearts of the *fathers* that will first turn toward the children, not the other way around. I believe leaders have mistakenly labeled those with a "runaway spirit" as having an orphan spirit. While it is true that an orphaned heart may run away, more often than not the motive behind one doing this is rooted in self-preservation, not blatant rebellion. In their hearts, they felt abandoned (even if this is not physically the case), so they felt that they had to run away to protect themselves.

If a person with an orphaned heart is placed in a position of leadership, they will be self-centered and struggle to mature as a father or mother. They will also struggle severely with suspicion and paranoia. The enemy will likely creep in and have a field day here, but the power of God is stronger than any powers of darkness.

My family and I currently reside in Hamilton, Alabama, where we attend The Ramp Church. This community of believers was brought together through The Ramp's conferences and youth movement, which spurred a revival that began nearly twenty years ago and continues to this day. Thousands and thousands of teenagers (and older folks) have come through the doors of The Ramp to attend conferences aimed at awakening a generation at the most crucial time of their development. A few years back, The Ramp launched a school of ministry and I am happy to say that my oldest daughter, Kalyn, was the first student to ever be accepted. My oldest son, Josiah, is also a graduate and currently serving as a third-year intern.

The Ramp was originally founded by Karen Wheaton. Many of you may know her as a Gospel singer who appeared on many Christian television networks in the 70s and 80s. During this time, she also traveled the country and served alongside many well-known ministers. Then, in the latter part of the 90s, while spending time in her hometown, she began to take notice of the young people in her community. The Lord allowed her to see their severe spiritual needs, and in 1998 she made the decision to move back to Hamilton to reach the youth of her community.

This is how The Ramp began. Not with an astounding supply of resources, or even with a blueprint and plan. It was the heart of a spiritual mother engaged with the heart of the Father that created the necessary synergy needed to serve as a catalyst for revival. It was the heart of a mother engaged with the heart of the Father that has sustained this move and grown it to where it is today. Rick and Karen Wheaton-Towe now oversee the operations here at The Ramp, and to this day it is astonishing what God is accomplishing through them. Obviously, there are many moving parts of this ministry, and it is not solely based on the efforts of one person, but it began when a mother's heart emerged.

This is a picture of what we need all over the world in this hour. Not a replica or duplication of a particular ministry, but spiritual mothers and fathers being compelled by the Father's love for his sons and daughters. If you look at many of the truly successful ministries throughout the earth today, you will begin to see this model of the hearts of mothers and fathers turned to the children, and the hearts of the children turned to the mothers and fathers. Many of these young men and women have gone on to establish ministries of their own, which follows the design of God for His work to continue from generation to generation.

DO NOT SEEK THE HONOR THAT COMES FROM MEN

If you want to see revival, renewal, outpouring, transformation (or whatever you desire to label God's work), this is surely a key—not seeking the honor that comes from men. In fact, I believe it is crucial that we get this.

> Speaking to the Pharisees, Jesus said, *"I do not receive honor from men. But I know you, that you do not have the love of God in you. I have come in My Father's name, and you do not receive Me; if another comes in his own name, him you will receive. How can you believe, who receive honor from one another, and do not seek the honor that comes from the only God?"* (John 5:41-44).

Wow! Our potential downfall is described in this passage. We all starve for affirmation. We all want the approval of others. I, too, have been guilty of this at some level, as few—if any—of us have "arrived."

It is true that we all have a *need* for affirmation. However, this need must not become an unbridled lust for the praises of man. When it does, it will begin to affect the motives of our hearts. We will know we are living for the praises of men when their criticisms have more of an impact on us than they should. Jesus experienced a considerable amount of ridicule, but it did not stop Him from doing what He saw the Father doing and saying what He heard the Father saying.

I'll take this a step further and say that *why* we do what we do is more important than *what* we are doing. Are we seeking the honor that comes from God and willing to lay down our lives for His Kingdom, or are we too caught up in receiving the honor of man for our own personal gain?

To illustrate this further, let's take a look at the story of the rich young ruler:

> Now as He was going out on the road, one came running, knelt before Him, and asked Him, "Good Teacher, what shall I do that I may inherit eternal life?"
>
> So Jesus said to him, "Why do you call Me good? No one is good but One, that is, God. You know the commandments: 'Do not commit adultery,' 'Do not murder,' 'Do not steal,' 'Do not bear false witness,' 'Do not defraud,' 'Honor your father and your mother.'"
>
> And he answered and said to Him, "Teacher, all these things I have kept from my youth."
>
> Then Jesus, looking at him, loved him, and said to him, "One thing you lack: Go your way, sell whatever you have and give to the poor, and you will have treasure in heaven; and come, take up the cross, and follow Me."
>
> But he was sad at this word, and went away sorrowful, for he had great possessions. ~ Mark 10:17-22

This man thought his works would surely qualify him, so Jesus purposely raised the bar. There is another point to this story I want to make, one that is easy to miss. The rich young ruler wanted to receive Jesus' approval for his achievements, and perhaps wanted recognition from the crowd as well. We may desire approval for our perceived goodness; yet, according to Jesus, there is no one good but God (Mark 10:18 or Luke 18:19) and He accepts us apart from our works.

What was the young man seeking? Is it possible that he was really wanting the honor that comes from man? Was he not merely seeing Jesus as a good Rabbi when he approached Him, and not the Christ? Was he offended when Jesus would not accept his compliment when he called Him "good?" Did Jesus ask too much of him? What caused him to walk away sad?

I would like to propose that he was upset that his life was not affirmed and honored as it was, that Jesus' perspective of him was lower than his perspective of himself.

There are two things to glean from this. The rich young ruler saw Jesus as a popular man who was on the cutting edge of things. He did not realize that it was not a celebrity that stood before Him, but the Son of God Himself!

When we seek the honor that comes from men, "How is it possible for us to believe when we receive the honor that comes from one another, and reject the honor that comes from the only God?" (John 5:44, paraphrased). These are Jesus' words, not mine.

The Lord spoke to me today, and I am clear that this is a key, undermining force that is at work against the Body of Christ today. I felt the Lord speaking: *The amount that you seek honor from one another will reveal the effects that ridicule works against you.*

Here we stand at a crossroad. Will our hearts be held hostage by the same things that caused the rich young ruler to walk away sad? Thank God for His grace, as He calls us to cross this threshold. It will require that we humble ourselves. We must seek the honor that comes from God alone, no matter what it costs us. I cannot write these words without a tremble in my own heart. I do not mean this to be taken as a condemnation, but as a simple fact—a fact that we vigorously ignore. We don't want to hear this, because many of us are guilty of it.

We often hear things like, *You need to network. You need to connect with others; that's how doors open.* However, when we seek this, are we not seeking the honor that comes from men for our own gain and rejecting the honor that God alone can give? Think about it.

Every blooming generation has always been able to see the blind spots of the previous generation. All maturing generations have always seen the pitfalls that cause history to repeat itself. These generations need to embrace the wisdom flowing from each other, whether it seems worthwhile or not.

> "Behold, I will send you Elijah the prophet Before the coming of the great and dreadful day of the Lord. And he will turn the hearts of the fathers to the children, And the hearts of the children to their fathers, Lest I come and strike the earth with a curse." ~ Malachi 4:5-6

We have been able to wink our way through many things, but we now stand at a crossroad. Now is the time to be sober-minded and take heed to what the Spirit is saying. First, we must humble ourselves and receive what God is speaking. We must measure our hearts against this word. We must turn our hearts to Him and ask for Him to quicken this word in our hearts. We must surrender.

If you see that you have been blind to this, repent! Adjust your thinking. Ask God to reveal to you the joy that awaits you on the other side. Allow God to transform you until you reach the point where you are not satisfied with the honor that comes from men, but instead hunger for the honor that comes from God and God alone! When we cross this threshold in our hearts, a new level of God's glory will be revealed through us, as all of creation groans for the sons and daughters of God to be revealed (Romans 8:19).

SUBMISSION TO AUTHORITY

Too often, we judge a person's ability to be obedient and faithful to God by how well they submit to us. We do the same thing with their authority as well, only judging it as legitimate if we have placed our seal of approval on it. Certainly, how a person responds to those in authority can reveal whether or not they have a submissive heart. However, if we were to judge Jesus by these standards, He would've failed in every area when He began His ministry.

Scripture tells us that Jesus was submissive to His parents while He was growing up. However, when He began His ministry, He stepped into the role and authority He was designed for. The Pharisees did not like this, because He did nothing to seek their permission or approval. Instead, He was obedient to His Father and committed to fulfilling His Father's purposes. His obedience was not measured by the religious leaders of the day, but by God alone. When the Pharisees realized they had no control over what this "troublemaker" did or said, they resorted to discrediting Him and, ultimately, killed Him.

When it comes to submitting to authority, it is far more important to be obedient to what God has spoken to you personally, even if it means people or a group reject you. This is not to say that man's authority has no place in our lives, nor does it mean one should "go rogue" and refuse to submit to the leadership of a local assembly. I believe that one should become a member of their local church, and doing so places one under authority. What I am saying is that you can be "all in" to the mission of your church, submit to every leader and join in on everything they desire to accomplish, and still never know Christ on a personal level or accomplish what He called *you* to do.

Submission and authority in the Kingdom of God has more to do with discerning the Body than a designed system that is really no different than any common business model. When Jesus stepped into ministry, He fully expected His sheep to know His voice.

Do not be intimidated by accusers, nor be afraid to endure the fires of their accusations. For when you arise from the ashes, you will be unafraid and all of hell will tremble.

DO NOT BE SWAYED BY THE CROWD

I once heard the Lord speak this to my heart: *Anytime the spirit of the mob rules, the spirit of Barabbas is released and the innocent will suffer.*

This is another big key we must grab ahold of. It is related to the chapter you just read, but I want you to catch the dynamics of the evil that exists in following the crowd. Through social media, we live in a culture where we pay attention to trending stories, trending opinions, trending ways to do things, trending thoughts—trending whatever; you get the picture.

However, if you follow Christ, there will be times you may have to walk alone, or with few companions. This is because there is a power that is released through the agreement of a crowd. We can see the good side of this power in church services or other corporate meetings, but the dark side is often revealed in the media, on social media, in social structures, and in institutional gatherings. A crowd can release life or destruction, and the individuals within a crowd tend to follow the whims of the crowd. This is why the people of Jerusalem joyfully welcomed Jesus on Palm Sunday and shouted, *Crucify Him!* on Good Friday. They were following along with whatever was popular in a given moment.

After this spirit had overtaken the crowd, Peter began to feel the weight of being one who followed Jesus. In a short window of time, he found himself denying Him three times. The crowd can create an intense pressure that can get the best of even the most committed followers of Christ. Without the power of God working in us, we can succumb to it as well. We may not deny Jesus outright, as Peter did, but there are times when we do this without even realizing it. If we were honest, we would see that almost all of us have denied Christ in one way or another.

Jesus had numerous chances to walk with the crowd, but chose not to. One example was the time when there was a woman caught in the act of adultery (John 8). Several men brought her to Jesus and told Him how she had broken the Law. They then gathered a crowd to stone her, because, according to the Law, she was indeed guilty. But as true as the accusations were, and as horrible as what she did was, she needed something else in that moment. She needed someone who would stand with her when the accusations were flying at her. She needed someone who would stand with her until all her accusers were gone. She needed an advocate.

So often, we believe we are serving God and humanity by proclaiming what we think is truth, mixed with a spirit of accusation, instead of being what a person needs most in the moment. Jesus did not instruct the woman to do anything until her crowd of accusers had left. It was only then that He said, "Go and sin no more" (John 8:11). In that moment, God, through Jesus, was reconciling this woman to Himself, not holding her sins against her (2 Corinthians 5:19).

It is who Jesus is to us when we know we are caught in a sticky situation that makes His grace so amazing. In those moments, we know we have seen the Messiah. His words are clear, concise, and cut through the confusion the enemy loves to create in our minds.

The spirit of religion loves opportunities to "make an example" out of others in order to promote itself as "the one to follow." This spirit causes one to gather a crowd around them to make it appear as though their decisions are made "in a multitude of counselors." Then, they take a stand in what they believe is righteous indignation, only to leave a trail of casualties in their wake. In fact, the bigger the crowd they can gather to agree with them, the more justified they feel "in their own eyes" for their ungodly actions.

The question we have to answer is this: *Are we willing to be the one who stands with Christ, or are we going to be part of the growing crowd of accusers?* Perhaps this is the narrow way Jesus spoke of.

THE PROCESS

We are built on the foundation of the apostles and prophets, but it is also true that we are *being* built. All things that pertain to life and godliness have been deposited in us, according to 2 Peter 1:2-4. This treasure of His glory at work within us is transforming us. "It is finished," as Jesus said; yet we are being finished through our walk with Him, as we become more consciously aware of that which He has finished—who we are in Him, and who He is in us.

I'm reminded of the few years I spent working in the timberland business all over the Southeastern United States. During this time, I saw many plots of land that were previously used for coal mining. There is nothing uglier than land that is in the process of being mined, as bulldozers carve up the hillsides and muddy lagoons fill with rainwater. Yet, beneath the surface, something precious and valuable is being extracted. This is especially true in areas where gold is mined.

Once the area has been fully mined, the mining companies are responsible for restoring the land. This typically leads to it becoming even more beautiful than before. Pristine lakes now replace muddy lagoons, and grassy knolls lined with trees replace machine-torn hillsides. I have always been amazed at how well mining areas can be refurbished, and the same principle can be applied to our lives as well.

"I indeed baptize you with water unto repentance, but He who is coming after me is mightier than I, whose sandals I am not worthy to carry. He will baptize you with the Holy Spirit and fire. His winnowing fan is in His hand, and He will thoroughly clean out

THE PROCESS

His threshing floor, and gather His wheat into the barn; but He will burn up the chaff with unquenchable fire." ~ Matthew 3:11-12

In this passage, the Lord speaks of separating the wheat from the chaff. In other words, He separates the precious from the vile, just as gold miners do. The process may look ugly. It may require everything on the surface being torn apart. We may not even recognize that Jesus, the Author and the Finisher of our faith, is separating the precious from the vile. Though the landscape may look ugly, the miner—God Himself—will restore us after the process is complete. Our role is to simply surrender to the process.

What often trips us up is our tendency to value the landscape more than the precious metal that is being brought forth beneath the surface. If we focus on what God wants to form in us, He will take care of the things on the surface. He will not only restore us; He will make us stronger and more beautiful than we ever were before. If things don't look like you hoped they would, take heart and look to Jesus, the Author and Finisher of your faith. He is the miner of the treasure in your heart, and He takes full responsibility for your restoration.

If this process is at work in our own lives, we must also understand that it is at work in those around us as well. We often don't discern when people are in the process of being finished, which can lead us to become frustrated with what we see on the surface in their lives. If we don't discern the Body correctly, our reactions can cause harm to those who are in the process of being finished.

THE PURPOSE IN THE PAIN

I, as well as many others, have released prophetic words of a new season we are stepping into corporately, where many who have been waiting for years to fully step into their calling and destiny are being released. While going through this extreme period of waiting, many have endured relentless hardships of various kinds—some from external persecution, and some of their own makings. (I know this is what I have gone through in my own life.) There is a heavenly purpose for this. While it may seem that we have endured injustice, which we have at times, it has been used by design for a divine purpose and our ultimate good.

We simply don't know who we are in distress until we are faced with distressful circumstances. Sooner or later, we will all face difficulties. When we do, our true selves will emerge. This has been true throughout all of human history, and it's true today as well.

Whether or not David knew he was a giant slayer, he wasn't *known* as one until he actually faced Goliath and took him down. So many of us who are Christians argue about whether or not God allows certain things in our lives for the purpose of teaching and training us. Obviously, God did not lead Goliath to attack His people, but I have a hard time believing that David's encounter with Goliath was not orchestrated, and I also believe that God prepared him in advance for that moment. The Holy Spirit is our teacher in all things. It was the encounter and overcoming of the giant that made David a national and biblical hero.

Even Jesus was sovereignly led by the Spirit into the wilderness to be tempted by the devil, and it was in this moment that He overcame the evil one. Later, in the Garden of Gethsemane, He overcame His own

THE PURPOSE IN THE PAIN

flesh when He said to the Father, "Not my will, but yours be done" (Luke 22:42). Then, on the cross, He overcame death.

God's divine purpose is to bring us to a place where we can endure the most difficult of circumstances and come out on the other side with a soft and tender heart that is yielded to God's Spirit. This is where we are tested, as many are hardened, not softened, by adversity. God desires to develop in us a heart that is tender toward Him and His people, a heart that is familiar with the sufferings of Christ and has learned obedience through suffering (Hebrews 5:8). This heart is full of a level of mercy and compassion that did not previously exist, and is able to release grace and understanding to those who are still in the process. It is free from arrogance, anger, resentment, and animosity toward others—from one's self to one's enemies. When we reach this place, we will know that it is God who brought us there, just as Joseph came to the place where he saw God's work in his brothers' wicked plan to throw him into a pit and sell him into slavery (Genesis 50:20).

It is vital that we understand that God uses difficult and painful circumstances to form us into His image, so we can walk through seasons of difficulty with a resolve to keep our hearts tender and pliable, like the new wineskin we have become. In these seasons, we will see just how strong the hand of God is in our lives. His ability to keep us through trials is unparalleled. We will come out stronger than ever before, with a fresh and deeper understanding of the ways of the Kingdom. We will develop a more intimate relationship with Jesus as we come to realize that He is Lord and we are not, just as John the Baptist did (John 3:30).

I completely understand that you may have been tested in these things repeatedly. You may feel like the trials will never end. I get it. I've been there. However, I have come to learn that whatever battles I fight are for my ultimate good, and the good of those I am able to minister to. I have learned that it is God who is for me, not against me, in the fight, though sometimes it can feel that He is working against me.

We won't truly understand brokenness without being stretched beyond our breaking point. Here, we will be confronted by our own offenses, and we will have the choice to remain offended or trust God with our lives. Offense comes when we don't get what we believe we deserve, or when someone else gets what we believe *they* don't deserve.

It's like that moment in John 21:18-23, when Jesus told Peter what he would suffer, how he would glorify God even in death. Peter's initial response was to look at John and say, *What about him?* Jesus answered, *"If I want him to remain alive until I return, what is that to you? You must follow me."* Jesus is taking us beyond ourselves into the place we never dreamed we could walk. When we say, "Here I am send me," we too will be humbled under the mighty hand of God.

Nothing reminds us more of the importance of humility than our limp (Genesis 32).

Nothing teaches us more about grace than the thorn God doesn't remove (2 Corinthians 12).

I never fully appreciated God's "rod and staff" until I experienced the green pastures and still waters. In that moment I could truly say, "Your rod and your staff, they comfort me" (Psalm 23:4). In that moment, circumstances were irrelevant.

Does this mean we are not to be bold? Not in the slightest!

> If anyone speaks, let him speak as the oracles of God. If anyone ministers, let him do it as with the ability which God supplies, that in all things God may be glorified through Jesus Christ, to whom belong the glory and the dominion forever and ever. Amen. ~ 1 Peter 4:11

God's Spirit makes us strong and of good courage, believing that all things are possible. This enables us to boldly stand with the oppressed and afflicted at our own cost. The Spirit leads us to everything God has called us to be: Purchased but free, gentle but bold, strong in weakness, upright in corruption, a lion and a lamb, confident in our King, kind but honest, joyful in the face of trials, the head and not the tail, more than a conqueror, heirs of His promise, sons and daughters, a betrothed bride,

THE PURPOSE IN THE PAIN

fearless in troubled times, full of faith, established by His grace and by His goodness—forever and ever, amen!

On a side note, a strange thing happened to me last year. Our cat wanted to go outside, so I let her out. As I did, I noticed a beautiful, Monarch butterfly flying about. It landed on a small wildflower and, within moments, my cat ran over and pounced on it.

Now, I grew up hunting and fishing, and I normally hold no opinion when things of this manner take place in nature. At the same time, I knew this butterfly had been through the long process of transformation in a cocoon, as it went from being a caterpillar into something great. I felt horrible that a creature that had been through such a long process and just begun to fly was suddenly destroyed without warning. I found myself running out into the yard in an attempt to rescue this butterfly from my cat, but I was too late; my cat had already torn the butterfly's wing.

Then the Lord began to speak to me: *Be careful how you love and touch those who have been through the suffering that occurs in the process of transformation.*

I felt a deep sadness and sense of sobriety in these words. As soon as I heard them, I knew He wasn't just talking about butterflies, but those who have endured much pain and suffering to become who they were called to be. This is the journey for many of us. We may go in looking like a caterpillar, but we come out transformed into a brand-new creature, with a new world to discover.

We must be careful about what comes out of our mouths when we see others who are following after Christ and learning to fly. Our opinions are really not needed, nor are they that important.

GOD SEES YOUR TEARS

Sometimes, a tear is the greatest offering we have to give to God. Not tears of self-pity, but the tears that come when you know deep down you've run out of road, only to look up and see your loving Father gazing intently at you with kindness in His eyes. These kinds of tears are worth their weight in gold because they contain the burdens of broken promises, betrayal, accusations, hurts, loss, and lies that our hearts have been assaulted with, even the things which we have brought upon ourselves. These tears move the heart of God; they are the expressed prayers of the contrite and brokenhearted. Words cannot do them justice.

He is not mad at you. You are indeed the apple of His eye. You are His prize possession, and He knows everywhere you have been, and everything you have been through. Yet, His love for you has never ceased or waned. He is the One who never leaves you. He never forsakes you. He is always the happiest when he sees you running to His arms, no matter where you've been or what you have done. He is your Father, and as much as you love your children, He loves you more.

He is the Author and Finisher of your faith. His word is the last word concerning you. His goodness to you will not be overcome. His grace to you will not be thwarted. You are His beloved child, and as with any Father, He is your protector. He is your rear guard. He brings the balm of healing and the oil of gladness to you. He is your covering. He is your loving Father who fearfully and wonderfully made you. Who knew you before you were in your mother's womb. You are His promised land, and He is your promised land. To Him be the glory forever and ever. Amen.

Enduring Whispers in the Night

To live so far away from home,
Imprisoned by the great unknown.
Grieved inside my soul does bare,
Relentless gnawing, deep despair.
I sit among the thistle thorn,
They mock me sure so deep with scorn.
The more I love the more it hurts,
No shortcuts left for me to skirt.
The more I speak the more they sigh,
I speak what's true, I do not lie.
It seems I'm not so understood,
Perhaps myself I wish I could.
Mysterious wisdom so obscure,
Denies me not, so true and pure.
Soon one day I will walk free
Of house arrests identity.
A slave of sorts, a prisoners' lair,
It seems that I'm beyond repair.
I hold the answers for the world,
Yet cannot spoil my little girls.
With all the wisdom given me,
I cannot give my sons their need.
For all the knowledge I bestow,
I find my wife beneath the load.
So what is this a man like me?
A man so tired, a man so weak.
Holding on with little might,
He can't quit now, he has to fight,
The fight of faith beyond the sight
Enduring whispers in the night.
Does Don Quixote ride again,

THE HOUSE THAT JESUS BUILT

Fighting windmills in the glen?
Or am I truly stepping in?
Eternal battles we must win.
It all depends on who you ask,
If I'm a fool or just an ass.
Perhaps I'm all or everything,
A narcissist who writes and sings.
Delusional perhaps insane,
Who could know of such a thing?
They must know something I don't know
Seems I walk against the flow.
I find myself sometimes amazed,
The irony of a thorny maze.
But go I will into the night
Holding on with little might,
I can't quit now, I have to fight,
The fight of faith beyond the sight
Enduring whispers in the night.

GOING LOWER STILL

Jesus prayed, "Father not my will, but your will" (Luke 22:42). We must pray this same prayer today. In fact, we need to proclaim many things along these lines, such as "Father, not my identity, but Your identity. Not my thoughts, or their thoughts about me, but Your thoughts about me. Not "my church," or "their church," but Your church. Not my ministry, but Your ministry. Not my children, but Your children. Not my family, but Your family. Not my body, but Your body. Not my name, but Your name." You get the idea.

God doesn't normally snatch our idols out of our hands. He expects us to deal with them when they are made known to us. As clear as they may become, they will become clearer still. We will visit these places many times in our walk, and the voice of God will always call us to go lower still. Humility is a school we never graduate from.

Having things in your life that you have not yet overcome doesn't necessarily mean that you aren't following God with your whole heart, though this is what the spirit of religion will tell you. All that junk does is make you feel disqualified so you will lay down and take the beating it would impose on you. It's a lie birthed in hell, and it's not who you are. The whole reason Jesus wants relationship with any of us is, first and foremost, because He loves us with everything He has and everything He is. The things we think disqualify us are the very reason why Jesus came in the first place. Your perfection is found in Him, not in yourself.

Trust God to be your deliverer, for He surely will. "Not by might, not by power, but by My Spirit says the Lord!" (Zechariah 4:6, paraphrased).

I KNOW WHAT IT'S LIKE

I have known what it's like to feel lost after proclaiming to everyone I was found. I know what it's like to have all the hope ripped from my heart, leaving me in a place of desolation. I know what it's like to be imprisoned by things that would have horrified and shamed me previously. I know what it's like to be humiliated beyond what I can bear on my own. I know what it's like to lose every material possession that would enable one to function, including a home, vehicles, and income for a prolonged period of time. I know what it's like for my choices to cause others to suffer loss and heartache. I know what it's like to have ongoing, disabling health problems that come to challenge the truth that Jesus came to heal and set free. I know what it's like to pray for God to take me in my sleep, because I didn't feel I could live with the dysfunction and the loss. I know what it means to suffer depression to the point of not being able to function. I know what it's like to be betrayed, denied, and written off. I know what it's like to be ignored and rejected. I know what it's like to think everyone would be better off if I was gone, because I once believed I was toxic.

Because I have been acquainted with these things, when I say that God, in His goodness, will meet you right where you are, I know from experience that He will. When you find yourself imprisoned (either physically or mentally), God will visit you. When no one will feed you, God will. When no one will cover you, God will. When no one will bring healing to your soul, God will.

If you feel as though you are an embarrassment to everyone around you, know that you are not an embarrassment to God! You are fearfully

I KNOW WHAT IT'S LIKE

and wonderfully made (Psalm 139:14), called according to His purpose (Romans 8:28), and your life has purpose as well (1 Peter 2:9, Acts 13:36). God loved you at your darkest point, and if you're currently in that place, there is nothing you can do to separate you from His love (Romans 8:38-39).

I have seen God's restoration. I have experienced His healing. I have experienced redemption, joy, peace, and righteousness—even in the midst of storms. We are now more than conquerors (Romans 8:37), and God is the Author and Finisher of our faith (Hebrews 12:2). What He has begun, He will finish. He alone has the final word concerning our lives.

God's goodness is not restricted by the boundaries of men or their religious traditions. There are no mountains that God can't tear down or walls He can't walk through. When He walks through the walls of the enemy, or perhaps the walls we have built around ourselves, He brings the entirety of His Kingdom with Him. He restores what cannot be restored. He heals what cannot be healed. He covers what cannot be covered. He accepts what cannot be accepted. He lifts burdens that cannot be lifted. Changes hearts that cannot be changed. He brings hope to the hopeless, faith to the faithless, courage to the fearful, a sound mind to the confused, and mends the brokenhearted, healing their wounds.

God will never deny, betray, rob, lie, or conspire to do anything to cause harm to His own. When He sees you, He sees you as one with Him in Christ (1 Corinthians 6:17). He will discipline His sons and daughters (Hebrews 12:6), but even in that, you will have confidence that you belong to Him. He is not fickle, He doesn't change His mind about you, your calling, or your purpose. He is for you, not against you (Romans 8:31). He is not mad at you, and He is calling you to come up higher. Turn your back on your failures. Turn your back on your losses and turn your heart to Him. He cares for you, and He will never leave of forsake you (Deuteronomy 31:6, Hebrews 13:5). Trust Him in the middle of your grief and your hardships, for they are very temporary (2 Corinthians 4:17). He will not leave you hopeless (Romans 15:13). He will not leave you orphaned (John 14:18). He is good, and He is true

(Psalm 33:4). Only God can raise you and enable you to stand above what lies beneath (1 Corinthians 10:13).

When you've lost everything that you hold most dear. When you've been betrayed, abused, overlooked, abandoned, sick, out-of-your-mind, blinded with grief, lied to, falsely accused, left for dead, traumatized, looked down upon, hated, and judged. When you don't care if you take another breath. When you find yourself questioning, "Is God even good at all?"

It is in this moment that God breaks in. In this moment, something seemingly small takes root and begins to grow within you, ever-increasing, burning brighter, becoming louder day by day, until the point where some miracle occurs and you stand up and proclaim the goodness and the majesty of God. In this moment, all hell may still be raging against you; yet, you fail to relent as you proclaim God's faithfulness. In this moment, all of Heaven stands to its feet and cheers you on as hell trembles and remembers your name, because of the power of Christ that is in you.

This is what it means to "know Christ and the power of His resurrection," which can only come from sharing in His sufferings. Rise up, warriors! Take hold of who God has made you to be.

> I want to know Christ—yes, to know the power of his resurrection and participation in his sufferings, becoming like him in his death, and so, somehow, attaining to the resurrection from the dead. Not that I have already obtained all this, or have already arrived at my goal, but I press on to take hold of that for which Christ Jesus took hold of me. ~ Philippians 3:10-12, NIV.

It Was On the Road to Jericho

It was on the road to Jericho,
It was on that road I laid.
So beaten down, unclothed and robbed,

I KNOW WHAT IT'S LIKE

Left to see the grave.
It was on the road to Jericho,
Wounded and afraid.
The same road all my friends would walk,
Who turned their eyes away.
There was a man who happened up,
Who saw the bloody splatter.
I didn't know him from my kind,
I guess it didn't matter.
He poured the oil, he poured the wine,
He took me to an inn.
He paid the keeper all the cost,
He said he was a friend.
He had an outcast pedigree,
Not one of earthen value.
In fact he's of the kind despised,
But me I sensed the power.
The power of unfailing love,
A stranger in the dark.
The power of unfailing love,
A Kingdom he was marked.
It was on the road to Jericho,
It was on that road I laid.
So beaten down, unclothed and robbed,
Left to see the grave.
It was on the road to Jericho,
Wounded and afraid.
The same road all my friends would walk,
Who turned their eyes away.
How many times could one pass by
And say, "He had it coming?"
How many times they walked around,
A blindness that was numbing?

THE HOUSE THAT JESUS BUILT

How many times could one point down
And say, "He's just a mess?"
How many times could one withhold
The grace that they confess?
It was on the road to Jericho,
It was on that road I laid.
So beaten down, unclothed and robbed,
Left to see the grave.
It was on the road to Jericho,
Wounded and afraid.
The same road all my friends would walk,
Who turned their eyes away.

BEING CONTENT

Let your conduct be without covetousness; be content with such things as you have. For He Himself has said, "I will never leave you nor forsake you."

So we may boldly say: "The Lord is my helper; I will not fear. What can man do to me?" ~Hebrews 13:5-6

Now godliness with contentment is great gain. For we brought nothing into this world, and it is certain we can carry nothing out. And having food and clothing, with these we shall be content. ~ 1 Timothy 6:6-8

Being content with what we have is a big deal. It doesn't just pertain to money, but it is certainly understood in this context. I am going to talk about what it means and what it doesn't mean.

How big of a deal is this? Well, we commit adultery because we are not content with such as we have. We riot in the streets because we are not content with such as we have. We murder because we are not content with such as we have. We change our identity because we are not content with such as we have. We lie because we are not content with the truth. We create other doctrines because we are not content with what Jesus said. We dismiss hell as a reality because we believe if God was as good as we are, then surely there is no hell. We worship other gods because we are not content with the One who was, and is, and is to come. Almost every evil we embrace is because we are not content with such as we have. Remember Adam and Eve?

Not only are we not content with such as we have, we're not content with what others have, either. We dismiss and run others off, because we are not content with such as they have. Without Christ, we will never be content with such as we have or what others have.

If there is anything to not be content with, it is the deep sleep we are in. It should be how little we contend for the presence of the almighty God who came to save us. How apathetic we are concerning an eternal judgment. How unconcerned we are with our own blindness. How prideful and arrogant we can be. If we really knew how much God's grace keeps us, we would never utter a bad word against anything so precious. The very fact we desperately need God's saving grace should be the one factor above all facts to know there is a wrath to come. If there was no wrath or a fallen condition, there is nothing to be saved from and there would certainly be no need for grace.

That's why Peter stunned the crowd that gathered during Pentecost with a blazing message to everyone.

> Then Peter said to them, "Repent, and let every one of you be baptized in the name of Jesus Christ for the remission of sins; and you shall receive the gift of the Holy Spirit. For the promise is to you and to your children, and to all who are afar off, as many as the Lord our God will call."
>
> And with many other words he testified and exhorted them, saying, "Be saved from this perverse generation." Then those who gladly received his word were baptized; and that day about three thousand souls were added to them. ~ Acts 2:38-41

Does this mean that God did not reconcile the world to Himself not counting people's sins against them? (2 Corinthians 5:19) No, He did, but only those who believe in Him who was sent will be saved.

Being content with such as we have keeps us positioned to be effective to do what we see Jesus do and say what we hear Him say. We remain in peace. We remain in faith. What this *doesn't* mean is that we make peace with disappointment. Though we are to be content even in disappointment, we don't make peace with the disappointing circumstances, thus giving them the power to define us and our lot in life. We are more than conquerors (Romans 8:37), even in those moments. We stay positioned in Christ, knowing that, suddenly, one word from God can change everything for our good. When God gives us a promise of who we are and what we will do, what we have or do not have in our current season has nothing to do with the promise being fulfilled. If we are experiencing a season that doesn't look anything like our promise, we must stay in peace, but not make peace with disappointment.

REST REVEALS OUR FAITH

When God reveals something (whether through Scripture, prayer, or a prophetic word) that He is going to do through you and for you, it should bring you to a place of freedom and rest, not a place where you fret and worry about how God will perform what He has revealed. You don't have to make things happen by trying to manipulate others to agree with what the Lord has said.

By grace you were saved through faith. By grace you are delivered through faith. By grace you are healed through faith. Everything that comes from God will be by grace through faith. The fulfillment of a genuine prophetic word spoken to you will be performed to you and through you by grace through faith.

Our warfare is to enter into the rest of the word as we declare our agreement. When we are tempted to doubt, we hold onto the word like a documented promise and declare, "God, You said this, I believe it, and that settles it." Then, we purpose our hearts to rest in it, enjoy it, and have faith in the One who is able to perform it.

Our rest, no matter the circumstances, indicates our faith. Our rest in Christ is a weapon of war.

THE ILLEGITIMATE AND UNLIKELY

The glory of God has always been to do the impossible through those who weren't capable, those who could never measure up, those who most would write off, those who have nothing to offer, those whose situations appear hopeless, those who want to throw in the towel, those whose reputation should disqualify them. What glory does God get in doing something through someone who knows it all, can do it all, has everything going for them, and is wise in their own eyes? If what we are saying and doing is not impossible for the likes of us, there is a good chance it's not God, but with God, all things are possible.

When Mary was carrying the Christ child, the entire circumstance appeared illegitimate, as she was a young woman carrying a child out of wedlock. The test for Joseph was to have faith in the legitimacy of her pregnancy being of holy conception, just as he was told by Mary and an angel in a dream.

At this time, there are many who are receiving divine impartations—pregnancies, if you will—a holy promise. The test for those carrying this divine pregnancy of the Spirit is the promise may appear illegitimate to some, thus inviting rejection and persecution. When God, in His wisdom, imparts His promise in the hearts of those we see as poor, miserable, blind, and naked, such as prostitutes, tax-collectors, and the like, and they suddenly begin following Jesus while still living imperfect lives, possessing little formal training from the institutional church nor a "covering," they are often viewed as illegitimate and thus ostracized.

So, the test for the Church in these days will be the same as it was for Joseph when Mary carried the Christ child. The Church will be challenged in the same way that Joseph was. Are we willing to be like Joseph and believe what Mary tells us? Are we willing to cover and bless the ones who may cause us to suffer reproach simply by means of association? True Fathers are willing to suffer the reproach of their sons. True husbands are willing to suffer the reproach of their brides. God has certainly been willing to suffer ours.

A FAILED TEST TO REMEMBER

In 1999, I left law enforcement and stepped out into full-time ministry. We were living in Eastman, Georgia at the time, and had three children. My wife, Christy, seemed to find these people in duress all the time, and would bring them to our home. She once found this woman on a bicycle at our local McDonald's and brought her home to stay with us for a few nights. This woman, who was from Michigan, had battled cancer, and was estranged from her daughter. However, she had become born again and wanted to see restoration in their relationship. She had decided to ride her bicycle from Michigan to Jacksonville, Florida in the hope that her estranged daughter would see her love for her and reconcile with her. Unfortunately, the effort was in vain, as her daughter rejected her. She was on her way back to Michigan, still on her bicycle. I am sad to say for me, all I saw was a crazy woman who had issues. A few years later the Lord spoke this to me, *Unless you can hear My wisdom in a homeless man, you will never turn the world upside down.*

I got it after that. I saw a fool, when the Lord saw love that compelled someone to ride a bicycle from Michigan to Florida. I was so arrogant, that while she was under my roof, I began to speak into her life as if I had what she needed. In reality, I knew nothing. I was the fool. All she needed was someone to see her love for her daughter and tell her everything was going to be okay. However, I felt that I knew exactly where she missed it. I felt that I had all the answers. But here's the truth: Is there anyone I would be willing to ride a bike from Michigan to Florida for? Clearly, I had more to learn in my understanding of what love looks like. Nearly fifteen years have passed since this event took place and I'm still learning from it!

Jesus came to earth and laid down His divine attributes, risking everything for us, with nothing promised. God loved us so relentlessly that He sent His only son. There were no guarantees that anyone would hear Him and believe, but He came anyway. He was so compelled by love and the hope of reconciliation with those of us who were estranged that He risked it all.

We have to see beyond our own glory and wisdom, or else we will become spiritually blind.

A SHOCKING AND PLEASANT SURPRISE

Years ago, when I was a deputy sheriff, we would often have state inmates work with us during the day. Their job was to take out the trash, wash our cars, help keep the office clean—whatever we needed them to do. We would pick them up around 6:00 or 7:00 each morning, and drop them off shortly before dinnertime. We called these guys "run-arounds," because that's essentially what they did.

There was one of these guys in particular that I was quite fond of. He was in prison for killing his wife and her lover after catching them in the act of adultery. I had him washing my patrol car one day when I noticed he was listening to Moody Broadcast Radio. As I was driving him back to the state prison, he thanked me for letting him wash my car at that particular time of day, as it allowed him to listen to Christian radio. I asked him if he was a Christian, and he replied, "Yes, sir."

I asked him what denomination he belonged to, and he told me he was a Jehovah's Witness.

Imagine the shock that I felt! I went on to ask if he believed Jesus was his Savior and he told me he did. He went on to share many things the Lord had shown him. I listened for a while, and was confident that Jesus was his Savior.

Why am I sharing this story? Because my religious buttons were being pushed! I was feeling the need to correct him, to tell him one couldn't be a part of such a group and belong to Jesus. All the while, the Spirit in me told me to leave him alone. This experience revealed to me that it is Jesus who is the Author and Finisher of our faith. We have to trust Him. Instead of speaking to him as a Jehovah's Witness, I began to speak to him as a brother, and the Lord manifested Himself through our conversations.

You see, the difference between manipulation and truth is this: Either we solely desire that people have an encounter with the true and living God, or we have an agenda that the person join our group. When I say, "our group," I mean the group of religious folks who decides who's in and who's out. You will find these folks in nearly every denomination or committee.

When we reach this place, where certain mandates and requirements must be met, it is nothing more than an indictment that we don't really believe that Jesus is the Author and the Finisher of our faith. Our argument is that people will ultimately be deceived. I get that, but even infants know who loves them and who doesn't. And believe me, if you are present, they will let you know.

I felt no need to try and convert this man from proudly proclaiming that he was a Jehovah's Witness, because I had settled in my heart that he had had an encounter with Jesus. It was obvious; the fruit was there. Does that mean I believe the Jehovah's Witness group is the way? No! Jesus is the way, the truth, and the life (John 14:6). However, I will say this: It doesn't matter what group you are affiliated with, if you have not had an encounter with the real Jesus, your group will be of no help to you, whether it is Southern Baptist, Charismatic, Pentecostal, or otherwise.

I have met Catholics who have had a revelation of Christ, and Charismatics whose hearts were as hard as a rock. When our agenda is for folks to have an encounter with the living God, our motives are as pure as they will ever be. When our agenda is to pull them into our group, we will often begin to manipulate, and we may begin to walk in the realm of "smoke and mirrors."

People need to know that the way has been prepared for them to have an encounter with a loving, gracious God who loves them just as they are. We who speak of such a God need to have faith that He is big enough to finish what He has started in these people.

A SHOCKING AND PLEASANT SURPRISE

Personally, I do not get uptight with other Christians if they don't believe exactly what I believe. I choose to believe that most are sincere and are living in the light that they have, just as I am. One day, we will all see clearly, but that day is not today (1 Corinthians 13:12). I myself believe some things I did not when I began this race, and I have discarded some things I once believed about my faith and found to be untrue, at least in the manner in which they were presented. I bet some of you have done the same. However, never have I doubted that Jesus is the way, the truth, and the life. Never have I believed there was any other way to the Father but through Him. Never have I believed that He did not die for our sins. I know that He alone is my Savior.

What I am saying here is that most everyone slinging doctrinal stones at each other believe these basic tenants and would die believing them. There is always one who is never satisfied—always. Trust me on this.

Until the Lord returns, no one is leaving here alive, and no one is going to get away with anything, either. You can rest on that. Who we believe in, for us, it is Christ, determines where our eternity will be spent. Yet, how we act and treat others will have an impact on our eternal reward, even when we end up with the Lord.

> Now if anyone builds on this foundation with gold, silver, precious stones, wood, hay, straw, each one's work will become clear; for the Day will declare it, because it will be revealed by fire; and the fire will test each one's work, of what sort it is. If anyone's work which he has built on it endures, he will receive a reward. If anyone's work is burned, he will suffer loss; but he himself will be saved, yet so as through fire. ~ 1 Corinthians 3:12-15

Jesus is building us individually, corporately, and globally. Not every encounter with a believer is for me or my group specifically. Some sow, some water, and some harvest. However, we can all be a blessing to our brothers and sisters, even if they belong to a different group than our own.

CHEER OTHERS ON

I have found that some people are far more forgiving of your sins than they are of your promotions. People with this type of heart condition are very territorial. Ironically, your promotion can be far more of a stumbling block for some than your sin. People in this condition cannot fathom the pleasure of God to bless His children. They find it hard to take into account what a person being promoted may have been through or suffered. Their thoughts are totally self-centered, and many times they do not realize it until someone is promoted who they don't believe deserves to be in the position given to them. Though these moments are designed by the Lord for the good of those with this issue, it does not always guarantee that they will adjust their heart posture and do what is right in the eyes of God. When they harden their hearts, all that matters to them is that the person who was promoted has invaded their territory and is now their enemy. This shouldn't be.

We must get to the place where we want everyone to make it, where we are able to cheer others on. I heard a great statement from Bill Johnson on this topic: "Brothers compete; fathers do not."

We must reach a point of maturity where this kind of pettiness stops. Especially between fellow children of God who are taking hold of the Kingdom of God. If we are honest, we will say that we really need to work on this ASAP. One way to exercise our faith in this area is to be intentional to cheer others on, even if they belong to a different group than we do or perhaps do not believe exactly as we do. This means that we are intentional to speak well of others even when they can't hear us. As many of our parents told us, "If you don't have anything good to say, don't say anything."

CHEER OTHERS ON

> Finally, brethren, whatever things are true, whatever things are noble, whatever things are just, whatever things are pure, whatever things are lovely, whatever things are of good report, if there is any virtue and if there is anything praiseworthy—meditate on these things. The things which you learned and received and heard and saw in me, these do, and the God of peace will be with you. ~ Philippians 4:8-9

How many of you want the God of peace to be with you? I know I do. According to this passage, this is the way if we practice these things.

Anyone can be an accuser of the brethren. That is how Satan himself is described. The only difference is when Christians do it, they do it in the name of the Lord. However, what does the enemy use to discredit Christians? Scripture, is it not? Isn't that how he tempted Jesus in the desert? He comes as an angel of light, I sure don't want him coming as me.

This doesn't mean we can never speak the truth in love to someone, but if you practice those things in Philippians 4:8, when you do have to say something, you will have already proven your love for them.

I love sports. I particularly love the Georgia Bulldogs football games. Friendly competition can be fun to watch. I love to watch events like the Olympics. The kind of competition I despise is the competition that comes from that which is birthed in pride, envy, angst, jealousy, and the like. Where elitism is the goal through the fight for control and manipulation. Nothing good will ever come from that, in fact, where this kind of strife exists, every evil thing is there.

> For where envy and self-seeking exist, confusion and every evil thing are there. ~ James 3:16

A father will not let this attitude hold any place in his home, for the sake of the others who live there. He will not tolerate it. The culture must be connected to and revolve around the father's heart. You will find the heart of God in this environment. You will find revival.

THE CONFRONTATIONAL CHRIST

When Jesus began His ministry on the earth, He didn't protest against the Romans. He didn't call others misogynists, racists, bigots, or supremacists. He didn't try to get politicians to pass laws so people would have to like Him. He didn't file a lawsuit against Pilate or Herod, or the Roman soldiers for their brutality. The only ones Jesus consistently rebuked were those who said they were of His Father but were not. The only property that He ever displayed violence against was in His own house. He did not walk in the evil wisdom of this age. Yet, the very essence of His being confronted all things. His very presence challenged the order of everything with a display of wisdom and power the world, and the religious establishment of the day did not—and still does not—understand.

We often say we belong to God, yet walk in the same wisdom of every generation that came before us. It's time for a reformation; it's time for a Jesus revolution. This is not a battle against the world, but a battle against our own ways of thinking. Before we concern ourselves with reviving the world, we need to see that we are the ones in need of prayer.

Jesus never planted a church, He planted Himself. The house Jesus built was not made by the hands of men, but by the hands of a homeless man, who happened to also be the Son of God.

> Then a certain scribe came and said to Him, "Teacher, I will follow You wherever You go."
> And Jesus said to him, "Foxes have holes and birds of the air have nests, but the Son of Man has nowhere to lay His head."

THE CONFRONTATIONAL CHRIST

> Then another of His disciples said to Him, "Lord, let me first go and bury my father."
>
> But Jesus said to him, "Follow Me, and let the dead bury their own dead." ~ Matthew 8:19-22

When Jesus came upon the scene to begin His ministry, He walked right up to certain folks He didn't know, fishermen and the like, and said, "Follow Me." When those men heard the Lord speak, they left everything and followed Him. They stepped out on a word from a stranger. Imagine what extraordinary authority and witness there must have been on His words, that men would leave their livelihoods and simply go. Jesus fully expected that when He spoke, His sheep would know His voice. He expects us to know Him and know His voice. This is what it means to have relationship with God.

When Peter stepped out of the boat and walked on water, he did so saying, *"Lord, if it's you, tell me to come to you on the water." Jesus replied saying, "Come."* Peter stepped out the same way he did when he began his journey with Jesus, on the word that Jesus spoke to him.

This is how the Spirit builds the house. He speaks clearly, and we respond. The measure that we respond in faith determines the measure to which we receive and benefit. That which seduces us from doing what we hear God say is the same as what seduced Eve in the garden; it is the enemy's voice saying, "Did God really say…?" This thought has corrupted us from the very beginning, and it continues to do so today if we allow it.

One thing the enemy commonly uses to corrupt our hearing is to create chaos in our lives that chokes out the word of God, making us dull (Mark 4:19). Often, this happens through every day, legitimate concerns. When magnified, these can take the place of God in our lives. When this happens, we find ourselves like the ones who were traveling with Saul of Tarsus. When the Lord appeared to him and spoke clearly, his companions heard the sound but didn't see anyone (Acts 9:7).

Perhaps one of the easiest ways the enemy corrupts our response to what we hear is our own ambition, envy, jealousy, self-centered selfishness, and competitive nature. All of these issues are actually rooted in pride and the fear of what men will think of us. When the Lord speaks in the presence of those with these types of issues in their hearts, if they are not absolutely offended by the notion, their response will be more concerned with how what He said will affect them in a negative way. Have we not all experienced this to some degree?

Jesus was very confrontational with those who claimed they were His but walked in another spirit. I can't help but think if we heard anyone speak today to any group of men as He spoke to these, we would immediately think He was bitter. We would think He was angry and walking in the flesh. We would say there were areas of His heart that needed to be healed, and we would refer Him to a Christian counselor. We would think that He was taking His frustrations out on others; yet, He had no bitterness in Him. There was no shadow of darkness anywhere in His being. This isn't about legalism, this is about His willingness to expose legalism, law-mindedness, and the pride of men, all of which prevent us from receiving grace. It's not that grace has not been offered to us, because it has. However, these mindsets and conditions of the heart can prevent us from receiving it because we think we have no need of it.

> "You are of your father the devil, and the desires of your father you want to do. He was a murderer from the beginning, and does not stand in the truth, because there is no truth in him. When he speaks a lie, he speaks from his own resources, for he is a liar and the father of it. But because I tell the truth, you do not believe Me." ~ John 8:44-45

Yikes! Imagine hearing that at a conference!

> "You search the Scriptures, for in them you think you have eternal life; and these are they which testify of Me. But you are not willing to come to Me that you may have life."

"I do not receive honor from men. But I know you, that you do not have the love of God in you. I have come in My Father's name, and you do not receive Me; if another comes in his own name, him you will receive. How can you believe, who receive honor from one another, and do not seek the honor that comes from the only God?" ~ John 5:39-44

Wow! It almost seems as though Jesus woke up on the wrong side of the bed, does it not? Imagine if your pastor laid that on someone in your presence, or even on you!

Even though it is true that we are under a new covenant, if we believe that these heart conditions that Jesus confronted no longer exist, we are delusional. Yes, Jesus spoke these words to those who were under the old covenant, but these heart conditions did not magically vanish after the cross.

Those who call out these things are often labeled as "bitter" or "wounded," however, I have found that this is not always the case. It is time we walk in greater discernment. Much of what we call "discernment" is not discernment at all; rather, we are fueled by suspicion. Suspicion can only "suspect," whereas discernment knows what it knows. Jesus did not walk in suspicion, He walked in discernment. Discernment is not having an opinion, it is the knowing of truth by the Spirit. Jesus calls all of us to lay down our suspicions so we can receive and walk in His discernment. Think about this.

"For the Father judges no one, but has committed all judgment to the Son." ~ John 5:22

"You judge according to the flesh; I judge no one. And yet if I do judge, My judgment is true; for I am not alone, but I am with the Father who sent Me." ~ John 8:15-16

"… as I hear, I judge; and My judgement is righteous, because I do not seek My own will but the will of the Father who sent Me." ~ John 5:30

> For we do not wrestle against flesh and blood, but against principalities, against powers, against the rulers of the darkness of this age, against spiritual hosts of wickedness in the heavenly places.
> ~ Ephesians 6:12

Our judgment is often not true discernment because we are so wrapped up in seeking the honor that comes from men rather than honor from God. In many cases, Jesus is the only one qualified to judge, and He does not seem as concerned with judging individuals as much as He is trying to help us see the bigger picture that our true battle is not against one another. Men are not our enemies, unless they have given themselves over to the enemy by an act of their will. Some have. Still it is consistent to say they can be delivered from this place. This is why we need true discernment. We are not here to wrestle with flesh and blood, but we certainly should war against the things that have taken flesh and blood captive.

> "… as I hear, I judge …" ~ John 5:30

Jesus walked in this discernment because He heard in "real time" with the Father. Therefore, when He spoke, what He spoke was true.

Make no mistake, it is God's goodness that leads us to repentance. Sometimes, the right word at the right time is a good thing, regardless of how others interpret it. There is no place for anything we speak to be motivated by envy, jealousy, covetousness, anger, wrath, selfishness, or anything else of the like. There is also no place of favor with those who shrink back:

> But we do not belong to those who shrink back and are destroyed, but to those who have faith and are saved. ~ Hebrews 10:39, NIV.

So, what is the Lord speaking to you today? What has He already spoken to you? We can pretend He didn't say anything to us, but only with ourselves and each other; we cannot pretend with God. It's better to say "yes" or "no" than to be found lukewarm and indifferent when God speaks.

THE HEART OF JESUS

Jesus showed His heart for us, long before He was crucified. He stood with the broken, the downtrodden, the ones considered trash, the ones thought to be the worst of the worst. In fact, it seems to me that the only ones He confronted belonged to the elite of society or religious circles; the very ones who were starving for a scapegoat, who needed someone to blame.

Jesus did not come to satisfy any thirst of His own. He was not out for blood, and He saw no need to blame anyone else. Rather, He laid His life down to satisfy *our* desire for blood and blame. You can trace this pattern of blame all the way back to Adam, who said, "It was that woman you gave me!" (Genesis 3:12, paraphrased).

Adam needed someone to blame. Jesus took away all our excuses by becoming our sacrifice. He literally became the sacrifice for us who needed someone else to blame, and He took our blame upon Himself. It was us who killed Him, not His Father. (Isaiah 53:4 says "*we* considered him punished by God, stricken by him ..." (NIV); it does not say that God punished Him!) Although it is true that He laid His life down (John 10:18), He did this *for* us, not against us. He took all the blame for all the wrath we had stored in our hearts. To do this, it was imperative in the end that we knew we had killed an innocent man. It's one thing to have murder in our hearts for an evil man who we feel needed to pay, but to know and realize that the murder in our hearts killed an innocent man suddenly changes everything. It is not until this moment that we examine ourselves. Truthfully, until we see that the murder in our hearts will surely spill over onto the innocent, we will not be shaken to our core as we should be. It is for this very reason that Jesus told the thief on the cross, "Truly I tell you, today you will be with me in paradise" (Luke 23:43, NIV). The thief knew Jesus was innocent. The problem is, many cannot see this simple point through their own lust for someone to blame. We want a scapegoat, but God gave us the Lamb. Jesus did take responsibility (for that which He did not even do!), and without this witness for us to observe, we never would.

We don't like to hear these things, but they are true. However, it requires a revelation of Jesus to change our hearts. He must do His work in us, as it is not enough for us to merely "know the truth" on an intellectual level.

If we have heard the truth and still feel the need for a scapegoat, perhaps we have only heard the truth in our *minds* and not our *hearts*. If we are still looking for someone to blame, there is a part of us, deep down, that believes Jesus' sacrifice wasn't enough. We want someone to pay, and fail to realize that One already did. Those who harbor the most anger toward God believe He owes them an explanation; yet, they ignore the murder in their own hearts.

The cycle goes on and on. It will never end as long as there is a lust in our hearts for someone to blame. When Jesus laid down His life, He took the blame. He took *our* blame. Is there another God one can name who would do such a thing?

DON'T SHOOT THE ARCHITECTS

You may remember me touching on this subject earlier in the chapter entitled *The Present Reformation Concerning Apostles*, but I sense the Lord wanting me to reiterate it more thoroughly. I have heard several leaders say that unless you have actually planted a church, or done some sort of "work," your revelation is irrelevant to them. To be honest, I could see where some may believe this to be a logical conclusion. However, I have found that this thinking is sorely misguided and disqualifying to those the Lord may be wanting to raise up.

The Lord has been speaking to me regarding this subject. You see, most architects never hammer a nail. They can envision and draw up plans and specifications, but they typically do not possess the skills to actually build their vision. Nor are they required to have these skills. They can hire those who do possess the skills, but they themselves don't actually build their vision. Does this make their plans any less legitimate?

If we have the mindset that a person with "blueprints" must have an established work to be taken seriously, we are likely to miss out on what the Lord is wanting to build. It would be like saying one shouldn't receive marital counsel from Jesus, simply because He was never married.

Scripture says that the people of the world who are wiser than the children of light (Luke 16:8). For example, a great artist may write songs; they may know exactly the sound and style they desire. But more than likely, before they record the songs, they will secure a producer, studio musicians, and a great mastering facility. The artist may or may not have any capabilities in engineering or producing. They may not possess the musical talent needed for each instrument. Yet, as we all know, without the artist's vision, there would be no substance for the engineers, producer, and studio musicians to build on.

When NASA plans to send someone to the moon, it takes a host of engineers to pull it off. Rocket scientists design the rockets, while engineers and mathematicians calculate arrival times. Yet, none of them will fly the rocket. None of them will step foot on the moon.

If you are wanting to build your dream home, I can bet you will want a great architect who can draw up your vision. I doubt you will be concerned with whether or not this individual can pour the concrete or hammer the nails themselves. You desire their ability to reveal the schematics.

The same is true in the building process of God's House—the Church.

Moses was given instructions for the Tabernacle and then gathered the artisans and craftsmen needed to accomplish the work.

Is it possible that rejecting those who have been given vision, blueprints, and plans stems from a place of insecurity and pride, rather than true wisdom?

I believe the Lord wanted to put His finger on this without condemning any individual or organization. He is building His house, so don't shoot the architects!

A WORD TO ARTISTS

God is calling His artisans to come out of hiding. The spiritual mothers and fathers in God's house need to engage with those who are artists. Many of these have been dismissed because, in the natural, they may only look like "artists" when God is actually using them in a prophetic manner to reveal His truth. They are some of the most important spiritual craftsmen the architects need in the building process. They possess the skills to express the invisible Kingdom and elements of the Temple of the Lord, and some are architects and builders in their own right as well. The world and the Church desperately needs what these folks have. When the artists are recognized, both the world and the Church can receive what the Lord is revealing through their artistic expression. We need them in order to more fully see who God is and what He is doing in the earth today.

Many of the greatest artists, songwriters, poets, and writers of this world are targeted by the enemy and have been taken captive in some way and brought into a place of "no man's land," where no one was meant to survive. Yet, somehow, they do. Though worn down, they return from this place and share what they found in the place of unbridled personal conflict. Through grief, sadness, and trauma they are caught between all that is beautiful and some sort of tragic cataclysmic destruction. By God's grace, they are able to bring back to us a glimpse of reality that we would never find in our normal experience. They reconnect us to our emotional selves while establishing us on a firm foundation. Think of them like David, who wrote some of the Psalms while living from cave to cave while Saul tried to take his life.

In the Spirit, many of these are forerunners, intercessors, and prophets. They are often the ones who discover the hidden treasures of the Kingdom. They see things other people walk by every day but are blind to. They can't help it; it is the way they were made. They pose questions and answers that sometimes seem absurd and offensive to our senses; yet, we are forced to consider and contemplate their expression. Much like the extreme fashion shows in Paris, with their outlandish presentations of different clothing styles. You can watch and expect for some dialed-down version of what initially seemed absurd to trickle its way down to the mainstream clothing lines, and you will recognize the source of inspiration. Though artists are not always the ones who carry their revealed expressions to the masses, they are often the ones who influence those who do. The artists who make the biggest impacts on society, as well as the Church, come to challenge the status quo rather than adapt to it. This is what forerunners do. Perhaps the Apostle Paul was one such as these, in the Spirit, to all of us.

Poets, authors, painters, sculptures, singers, and songwriters gained a lot of their wisdom through intense inner turmoil, confrontation, and conflict. Those gifted and even called with artistic genius are often broken, conflicted vessels. They possess a type of genius others do not, and the evil wisdom of this world and its cohorts will often seek to destroy them. Lucifer was an artistic angelic being, described as a musician having pipes built in his body. He wants to be worshipped because he has always recognized those who possess artistic expression, and he knows the threat that they pose. Perhaps this is why artists have always been in his crosshairs. In the Church, it is the spirit of religion that violently opposes artistic flow.

There have been many well-known artists in this world who were very talented, yet lived tragic lives. Brilliant in the genius in their artistic flow, yet they struggled to conform to what seems trite and shallow, even the things of a social nature. This can be seen or perceived as a form of arrogance, and it sometimes is. However, it can also be that these artists are introverts who interpret the world differently, and their aloofness is unintended—even unwanted by the artists themselves. They are not necessarily better, or more deserving, just different. What would the world be without them? What would the Church look like without them?

I remember the first time I heard the band Nirvana. They were so different from anything else that was out there at the time, to the point it shocked my senses. Their presentation was absurd but I couldn't quit listening to them. There was something about the music and expression that resonated, and I wanted to hear more. I didn't agree with all of their sentiments, but I could not deny the effect that their sound had on me as a musician. After Nirvana broke through whatever it is you have to break through, other bands surfaced that were obviously influenced by what Nirvana brought to the table. This is a great example of artistic diversity as well as a picture of the kind of influence and impact artistic forerunners can have on culture. No, Nirvana wasn't a forerunner for the Kingdom of God; this story was designed to create a picture that could be seen and understood. However, their musical style was so impactful in the world that it has influenced a lot of Christian musicians in the Kingdom as well. God uses everything for the good of those who love Him, does He not?

I hear the Lord saying, *Come forth, my expressions of glory. Come forth in the boldness of the Lion of Judah and the fire of Elijah. My chosen vessels of the expressions of My heart, come forth. I am raising up those who will see Me in you. Those who will hear Me in you. I am bringing forth new songs, new colors, new lines, new sounds, new shapes, new dances, new expressions of My glory. Brand new thoughts, never before conceived in the imagination of the hearts and minds of men. Come forth from the tombs of conflict and destruction with My treasures that you specifically carry for the brokenhearted and crushed. Take your place among the living and the dying and express My love and healing you now possess to all who have ears to hear and eyes to see. This is the day of the Artisan. This is your day.*

THE HOUSE THAT JESUS BUILT

The Artisan

The heart of the artist will yearn to reflect
What he sees and he hears, he wants to perfect.
Between the dimensions and forces at war,
Compassion and anger, an abstract abhorred.
Searching for something to just ease the pain,
In a world full of torture, doom, and disdain.
To create something beautiful, useful, and loved,
He searches for answers, eternal, above.
To set a clear picture of all that he sees,
The conflict is bringing him down to his knees.
But the greatest discovery for one so abused,
Is the knowledge that he is the Artisan's muse.
And only the Spirit of the Artisan knows,
From where the wind comes,
And where the wind goes.
For He is creating a masterpiece,
A satisfied heart in the work He completes.
A clump of pure mud on a Potter's wheel,
The relentless hands of the Artisan yields,
Constantly adding and cutting away,
Reforming, reshaping, and stretching the clay.
The painstaking process of being perfected,
May give the illusion of being neglected.
It's a secret place, the Artisan's loft,
His hands forging skillful, His voice is soft.
And only the Spirit of the Artisan knows,
From where the wind comes,
And where the wind goes.
For He is creating a masterpiece,
A satisfied heart in the work He completes.
When the artist knows he's the art being revealed,

A WORD TO ARTISTS

He yields to Artisan's hands and the wheel.
A realized canvas, with colors so lush,
Endures sitting still for the Artisan's brush.
And only the Spirit of the Artisan knows,
From where the wind comes,
And where the wind goes.
For He is creating a masterpiece,
A satisfied heart in the work He completes.

A WORD TO MY CHOSEN ONES AND THEIR SCOFFERS

(Taken from my previous book, *The Presence-Purposed Life*.)

To you that I have chosen, be blessed and be still and know My love for you. Hear Me, and see Me as I AM. I love you, and My heart longs for you. I AM for you. I chose you and have come for you, My brokenhearted ones, My bruised ones, My blind ones, My deaf ones, My lame ones, My poor ones, My imprisoned ones, My weary ones, My weak ones, My meek ones, My sick ones, My oppressed ones, and all who are lowly of heart. I have personally come to give you good news. To proclaim My liberty to you. Not to condemn you, but to give you My abundant life, according to My riches in glory. I have come to qualify those who have been disqualified. I have come to renew life where the enemy has drained it. It is My pleasure to do this because My Father wants this, and My food is to do His will.

I AM decides who He will be merciful to, and I AM decides who He will not have mercy for, because I AM He who sits on the throne. I AM He who sits in the throne room of grace, and I AM who decides who receives My grace. If you choose to receive My grace, it is because I chose you to receive My grace even before you were in your mother's womb. Many will scoff and say I have no right to speak this way, but I AM the one who decides who has what rights, and who speaks what way because I AM He who sits on the throne. Where were they when I laid the foundations of the earth? I choose whom I choose based upon My good pleasure and My love.

A WORD TO MY CHOSEN ONES AND THEIR SCOFFERS

No one knows who I AM but that is not revealed to them, and I AM giving Myself to the least. I give Myself to those I chose to call My own, and I call the lowly of heart to exalt, and exalt I will! I AM He who is here to raise up the ruined. I AM He who respects the shamed and mends the broken. I AM the advocate of victims and the only hope for offenders.

I will raise up those who have been declared dead in heart to be the instructors of the living. I will release My imprisoned ones to teach My freedom. I will remove the sickness off of the oppressed, and they will be a wellspring of healing. My lame will walk, and the wise will be confounded. I will remove the oppression from those who grieve, and they will mourn no more. I will keep company with those who are lonely, and set them in families. I AM He who gives liberty to the captives; I AM He who sits on the throne. I AM He who will sit among My chosen, as a refiner's fire, and I will purge them of their iniquities. I will purify whom I will purify because I AM He who sits on the throne.

Even now as I say these things, you who accuse continue to scoff. Excuse Me, who did you say that you were? You who would remind and instruct Me, on the day of your judgment, of your great miracles and prophecies—do I know you? For I say I never knew you, and you have your reward for what you have done. You call unclean what I have made clean. You call impure those I have made pure. You stalk the vulnerable and expose the weaknesses of My sheep. You need to pray that I would even grant you repentance, you arrogant ones. You enslave those who are already enslaved. You oppress those who are already oppressed. You steal from those who have already been robbed. You bruise those who have already been crushed. You make sicker those who are already sick. You place stumbling blocks in front of the blind, and you deafen the deaf with corruption. You cause the lame to trip, and the weak to fall. And somehow you do this in My name, and yet you have no shame.

Who are you again? I came to destroy the works of the devil, and now I am having to destroy your works as well. You who capture the imprisoned have been taken captive yourself to do the will of the spiritual wickedness you walk in. Take the eye salve of Heaven so that you might see again, because you tread very closely to the doorway of the decided fate of the evil one and his entourage.

THE SECRET PLACE

The most important key I can hopefully convey to you is this: The secret place is indeed the place where God begins to form His life in us. It is in this place where we hear His voice. He speaks softly and tenderly to our hearts; His words reaching the deepest parts of our being. Nothing is hidden, good or bad. He knows our greatest successes and darkest secrets and loves us consistently. This is the place where amends are made and heartaches are healed. It is a place of holy communion where we are one with the Creator of the universe.

What He speaks to us in secret, we are emboldened to shout from the rooftops. We are not just sharing words, but overflowing His attention and love. He holds us in His loving arms as only He can, as though we are the most important person in the universe. His love is faithful and true, and it purifies us of every stain from this age. When the pain is too much to bear, He comforts us and reminds us that we are in His eternal hands. Sin and death can no longer abound here. Their sting is removed, and new life begins where pain and death once reigned. Everything of eternal value starts here. This is the place where Life is conceived in us, which we carry until the day of completion. The secret place is where we learn who we are and why we were brought into this world.

As we grow in God, the secret place will become our home. I believe God is raising up a generation of people who will live in His presence, who learn what it means to abide in this place. It is a place where the impossible is indeed possible, a place where faith, hope, and love remain forever. It is a place where all who are weary find rest, a place where peace surpasses understanding. Here Jesus is revealed to us and we are revealed with Him in glory. Here the fog of war disappears and the sky over our hearts becomes clear, as we hear Him say, "Come up here, come up now, my beloved."

This is the place that was once behind the veil, but is now made available to us. Because of Jesus, the veil has been torn and we may enter by faith. We enter the secret place in meekness and humility, and leave with the vision of an eagle and the boldness of a lion. Perfection is not required; in fact, the thought that you might have "arrived" will prove to be an obstacle to entering this hidden life with God.

I must have more of Him. I have to hear His voice; I have to know Him. There is no other life I know. I have left everything and cannot go back, and I can hardly remember what was back there that I ever thought was so wonderful in the first place. Apart from Christ, I can do nothing. He is surely the Author and Finisher of my faith and I must hear His voice. He has changed everything—the way I think, the way I see, the way I define what is true and what is falsehood.

When I feel far from His presence, my heart cannot rest. As St. Augustine said, *My heart is restless until it finds it's rest in God.* I must look for Him; I must find Him. In reality, *I'm* the one who must be found— and He always seems to find me. When my heart is striving after lesser things, He brings me home and gives me rest.

The secret place is not only a place where we can find rest; it is a place where we can become a place of rest for others. 2 Corinthians 3:2 says we are becoming "living epistles" of Christ. In other words, when people come into contact with us, they see Jesus. If the tired and weary can come to Him and find rest, the same should be true about us. We should give others a living experience of Christ. When those who are in need of rest come into contact with you, are they able to rest in your presence? Will they find joy and peace? Will they find faith and strength for their journey? If not, what will they find?

In the secret place, we experience the heart of God and we become more like Him. We begin to see things through His eyes; His heart becomes our own. This is where revival is conceived. It begins in our hearts. We are the Bride of Christ. We carry His promise. He chose us for this. We were made for this. This is what revival, reformation, and restoration looks like!

A PROFOUND MYSTERY

How do you explain a mystery? How is it that God has reconciled us to Himself (2 Corinthians 5:18) and we find ourselves growing up in this reconciliation? How is it that we are built and are being built? How did He know us before we were in our mothers' wombs? (Jeremiah 1:5). How was Jesus born of a virgin? How are we able to see an invisible Kingdom that we cannot deny once we have seen it? How can we explain this to others? How are we to steward a mystery we cannot explain? (1 Corinthians 4:1). How is it that we proclaim the Kingdom of God is here and now, while it is also still to come? How can we speak with confidence about something of which we are only scratching the surface?

How can any of this be? It's a mystery. God has chosen us to enter the mystery of Himself. He expected us hear His voice and come to Him. He expected us to demonstrate the power of an invisible Kingdom in tangible ways. However, it is also consistent to say that we are not building the Kingdom so much as God is building us. This is a mystery in itself. In our own strength, apart from Him, we can do nothing (John 15:5). Yet, with God, all things are possible (Matthew 19:26). We may be helpless, but we have been empowered with a Helper—God's Holy Spirit is in us and upon us. There is a river flowing forth from our hearts (John 7:38). Can you see it?

You may well think I've lost my mind! In a sense, I hope that I have, for I know that one must lose their life to find it. (Matthew 10:39, 2 Corinthians 5:13) One must let go of their own ways of thinking, their lesser ways of thinking, to embrace the greater path that God invites them to journey on. When we renew our minds to Christ, we lose our minds for the things of this world. We are transformed as we behold mysteries we cannot comprehend. We are given the mind of Christ—a mind not of this world (1 Corinthians 2:16). A mind that propels us to embrace the mystery.

How can we weep when He weeps and laugh when He laughs? How do we say what we hear Him say and do what we see Him do? How do we pray with words we don't understand? (Romans 8:26). It's a mystery revealed to those who embrace it—to those who believe.

Does this make us mystics? When we embrace the Mystery that is not of this world, what else could we be?

This mystery is literal and ethereal, here and coming, within us and above us, connecting some while separating others, immovable and flowing. Can you explain it? Probably not, but He speaks for Himself. You can and will reveal it when you follow Him. God enables us through the very grace we will marvel over for eternity. What a mystery His grace is. Men are debating it now. Those born of God are embracing it with all their hearts as if their life depends on it—because it does. We were saved by it. We experience faith, hope, and love because of it, yet even these things are ever-increasing.

So, we know what we know, and we continue to learn and to know more. We catch further glimpses of who God is; we see more of the mystery only to find there is even more to discover. We hear God speak and we quickly learn that He doesn't stop speaking. How can this be?

Our God is alive, and we are growing up in Him. In reality, it is God who is growing us, for He alone can give the increase (1 Corinthians 3:6). The mysteries of Christ are being revealed in us and through us. We were born for this. We were His idea, in His heart from the beginning. We were not Plan B. This is a profound mystery.

I hear Jesus calling now saying, *Come away with me My love. Come to my table. Come to the wedding feast. Come away with Me and I will give you life. All that is made known from My Father I have and will make known to you. You are my beloved. You were one of the ones who would say "yes." You are one of the ones to demonstrate My love to this world. You are and you will be a mystery yourself revealed to others, because we are one and being made one, even as I speak. This is the mystery I have called you to.*

A PROFOUND MYSTERY

He IS

He is the earthen and divine.
He is the oil and the wine.
He is the theory and the equation.
He's the Master of creation.
Mysterious and obvious.
An anomaly to most of us.
To some surely known but thus,
To some He's anonymous.
He's a friend and a lover,
He was God undercover.
He is the first and the last.
He is the future and the past.
He's a rich man's Lord,
And a poor man's porter.
Shining bright as from afar.
Yet, close as His whisper in our hearts.
He never leaves or forsakes.
In my grief He partakes.
In my joy He shares,
In my crisis He cares.
He is joy unspeakable and full of glory.
He is the saga revealed in an unfolding story.
He's the wisest of wise, making weak men bold.
He's a heartwarming voice in a world grown cold.
He's a liberator and a captivator,
A reckoning and a motivator.
He's a servant and a King,
And good gifts He brings,
A beautiful fragrance and a flaming sword,
A dividing force, that brings one accord.
He is the truest of true to a dishonest heart.

THE HOUSE THAT JESUS BUILT

He is the bonding glue for the falling apart.
He's a consuming fire and many waters.
He's a still small voice and a trumpet with orders.
He's a drunk's best friend, and a fool's only hope.
He's a gambler's best bet, and a preacher man's Pope.
He is more than we perceive and more than we know.
A life giving nurturer tending our growth.
He condemns the accuser and justifies the condemned.
To the prostitute chastity exists once again.
He's the comfort that comes in the midst of tragedy.
He's the wisdom of life and perfecter of strategy.
He brings down the high place and raises the low.
For a heart turned to know Him, He'll search to and fro.
He's the world's greatest gift and the world's greatest need.
He's more than the universe contained in a seed.
And the greatest of miracles, perhaps most divine,
Is when He says I am His and proclaims He is mine.

CONCLUSION

There are two houses in our garden, just as there were two trees in the original garden (the *tree of life* and the *tree of the knowledge of good and evil*). One house is built by the Lord. The other house is built in vain. God is building and shaping us to be His house in an individual, corporate, and global sense. We are the Church. We are His Bride. He is the Author and the Finisher of our faith. Sometimes, the most significant choice we ourselves will make is choosing the life of God over mere knowledge about God.

We all know and see in part (1 Corinthians 13:9). None of us have the full picture, but this is my part that was conceived, carried, and delivered in the secret place of my communion with the Lord. At His prompting, I am sharing it with you. I pray that the words of this book have inspired you, revealed the Father's heart, and imparted to you the wisdom you need as we move into this new season. What a privilege to be alive at such a pivotal moment in history. I believe it is the Father's good pleasure and design for us to take part in such a moment.

Consider this: If love is not the motivating factor for what we are doing, if we know these things and grow in knowledge without an increase in love, it's all meaningless. Before we are able to love others fully, we must experience the Father's love for us, for we will only love our neighbor to the extent that we love ourselves (Mark 12:31). I am not talking about having an inflated ego; rather, I am referring to recognizing the love that God has for us and abiding in His love. The power of the resurrection is rooted in the Father's love for us. This love cannot be measured, but we catch a glimpse of it through Jesus and what He did for us.

> If I speak in the tongues of men or of angels, but do not have love, I am only a resounding gong or a clanging cymbal.
> ~ 1 Corinthians 13:1, NIV.

As I mentioned earlier, the last thing the Lord spoke to me on June 1, 2010 was, *Contend for My presence.* One moment in the presence of the Lord can do more to change your heart than years of prayer and study. We enter one way and leave transformed. We go in distressed and come out in peace. We enter in chaos and come out in order. I am not saying that there is no need to pray or study, because the Spirit will quicken the things you have studied and prayed about to your memory when He appears (John 14:26). However, we need God's presence more than we need our own discipline and reasoning. We need His presence more than the gifts He has given us. We need God's presence more than we need our own perceived integrity, and I believe it is impossible to walk in true integrity without spending time in God's presence.

When we receive the words that come from the Lord—whether by His Spirit or those He has sent to us—an extraordinary increase will occur in our lives. This is because we honor the person who was sent. Jesus said something profound in this passage.

> Jesus answered, "The work of God is this: to believe in the one he has sent." ~ John 6:29, NIV.

Some may say this passage refers only to Jesus, and this could be accurate. I say "could be," because while it is true Jesus was speaking of Himself, I believe He was also speaking for everyone who is sent. Did Paul not say, *I have been crucified with Christ; it is no longer I who live, but Christ lives in me; and the life which I now live in the flesh I live by faith in the Son of God, who loved me and gave Himself for me?* (Galatians 2:20). A simple reading of the Old Testament will show us that God has sent many folks to get His people's attention. He did so in the New Testament as well.

CONCLUSION

In the past God spoke to our ancestors through the prophets at many times and in various ways, but in these last days he has spoken to us by his Son, whom he appointed heir of all things, and through whom also he made the universe. ~ Hebrews 1:1-2, NIV.

I believe that God continues to send people with a word from Heaven to get our attention and bring us revelatory impartation. While Jesus is not physically present with us, He is alive in us through the Spirit. He speaks to us—sometimes for ourselves, and sometimes for the benefit of others. Receiving those who are sent is a huge deal to Jesus:

"O Jerusalem, Jerusalem, the one who kills the prophets and stones those who are sent to her! How often I wanted to gather your children together, as a hen gathers her chicks under her wings, but you were not willing! See! Your house is left to you desolate; for I say to you, you shall see Me no more till you say, 'Blessed is He who comes in the name of the Lord!'" ~ Matthew 23:37-39

In this passage, Jesus tells His audience they are not going to see Him again until they see Him in others. He is speaking of the fact that He is going to be with the Father, and to see Him, they will have to believe in the ones He has sent.

Whoa! That is why it is so important that we learn to discern the body of Christ. We must be able to discern those He has sent. When we see those who are sent as it is intended, we will see Him. Jesus told His own disciples, *when you have seen Me, you have seen the Father* (John 14:9). We don't win the lost by trying to prove the existence of Christ; we win the lost by *revealing* His existence. Blessed is he who comes in the name of the Lord.

What a challenge it has proven to be for us who believe to receive those who He has sent! We must see one another through the eyes of Christ and not our own opinions of who we think they are (2 Corinthians 5:16). The spiritual leaders of Jesus' day did not recognize Him when He walked among them. Ironically, the sinners did! I believe Jesus walks among us and speaks to us through unlikely people, but we cannot see Him because of our carnal nature, religious expectations, and pride have blinded us. Jealousy, envy, and coveting are also blinding, but those things are ultimately the fruit of pride residing in our hearts.

At the end of the day, when the house is built, we will know that it is the house that Jesus built. To Him alone will be the glory, the honor, and the praise, forever and ever. Those He sends will know and proclaim this. Amen!

I pray for everyone who receives this word, that you will lack nothing concerning your purpose in your pursuit of His will. That you will love others with the love you have yourself received. That you will experience new depths of communion with God as I have, and even greater depths. I pray that the unity of this communion will abound between you and all who are called by His name. I pray that you will know that God will withhold no good thing from you, and all of Heaven is behind you.

"He who has My commandments and keeps them, it is he who loves Me. And he who loves Me will be loved by My Father, and I will love him and manifest Myself to him." ~ John 14:21

What a wonderful promise from the Lord. He will manifest Himself to us. I pray that you experience His manifested presence and carry it with you. I pray you will know Him as your rear guard and the One who has prepared the way before you. I pray that you will know that your steps have been and will be ordered by Him. That you will find contentment in the process, all the while being impassioned by His love to take the next step. I pray for the breakthrough of this revelation in your life and the lives of those who hear your words. I pray blessings over each one of you, that you will see and know that you carry revival, reformation, and restoration in your heart even as you read these words. I pray this in love and in the mighty name of Jesus Christ, in whom all things are held together. Amen.

May God bless you and keep you.

SPECIAL THANKS

I don't want to let this opportunity go by without giving thanks to The Ramp Church in Hamilton, Alabama. This is our second time living here between ministry excursions, and we are very happy to be members of this community. One thing I personally love about The Ramp is their hearts are set to contend for the presence of God. The leadership here makes no bones about the presence of God being first and foremost. That should be the starting point for any group.

Our children have thrived here, and two of them are graduates of The Ramp School of Ministry. We deeply value this community of believers. If you are searching for a place that has a wonderful environment, particularly for reaching children and young people, I don't believe there is a place that does it any better than The Ramp in Hamilton, Alabama.

The painting seen on the cover of this book is called *To Write Plainly*. It was created specifically for this project. It was painted by a very talented artist and friend named Travis Binish, who is part of The Ramp community.

As I shared with Travis what this book is about, he caught the vision and expressed it in this painting. When I saw what he captured, I was stunned by his work. I am so thankful to Travis for the hours he put in to produce such a fitting and important piece for the cover of this book. I can now only hope that the book lives up to its cover.

If you would like to see more of Travis' work, you may visit www.travisbinish.com or follow him on Instagram (@travisbinish).

I would also like to thank my daughter, Tessa Mullis, for designing the cover itself. She is very talented as well.

ABOUT THE AUTHOR

Ken Mullis is an author, musician, songwriter, and poet originally from the state of Georgia. His first start in ministry was as a worship leader in 1986. Ken and his wife, Christy, set out into full-time ministry in 1999, ministering through prophetic praise and worship, speaking and ministering in churches thoughout the southeastern United States. They have been married for 30 years and have nine children and one grandchild. The Mullis family currently resides in Hamilton, Alabama where they are active at The Ramp Church.

In addition to *The House that Jesus Built*, Ken has written two other books, *The Presence-Purposed Life: A Journey to a Living Awareness of God*, available in paperback, and *Perceptions*, an eBook collection of poems, allegories, and other writings. Both are available on Amazon.com.

Ken shares his thoughts regularly on his Facebook page before they make their way into his books. You can follow along at www.facebook.com/Ken.Mullis.

www.ingramcontent.com/pod-product-compliance
Lightning Source LLC
Chambersburg PA
CBHW062103080426
42734CB00012B/2737